OVERCOMING YOUR BARRIERS

OVERCOMING YOUR BARRIERS

A Guide to Personal Reprogramming

Gerald W. Piaget
and
Barbara Binkley

NEW HORIZON PRESS
New Jersey

IRVINGTON PUBLISHERS
New York

iv

Library of Congress Cataloging in Publication Data   LC 8577 40   1985
Piaget, Gerald
Binkley, Barbara
Overcoming Your Barriers
(A Guide to Personal Reprogramming)
Includes Index
1. Behavioral Therapy
ISBN 0-88282-005-2 (New Horizon)
      0-8290-0438-6 (Irvington)

ACKNOWLEDGMENTS

Our sincere thanks to the hundreds of conference and workshop participants who contributed their time, energy and experiences to this book—and then demanded that we write it. The examples that enrich the following pages are theirs, not ours.

To Ryan, Megan, and Erin, who make the summers chuckle; and to Joan and Larry, who share them with us.

TABLE OF CONTENTS

FOREWORD

In the late 1960's, Gerry Piaget became my first post-doctoral trainee. He arrived at the Temple University Medical School in Philadelphia with an excellent academic and clinical background, to which I endeavored to add a wide range of behavioral procedures and effective problem identification strategies. Gerry proved to be a remarkably fast learner with distinct capacities for originality and creativity. He was also highly persuasive without being aggressive or overbearing. (For instance, he once enticed me to jump out of an airplane—with a parachute, thank goodness!) He also knew, and still knows, how to make and maintain leisure time for himself, and how to have fun.

After his internship year, Gerry took off for the hills of California, while I moved first to Yale and then to Rutgers, the State University of New Jersey. We met again after several years and found that, while we had worked quite independently, we had reached very similar

conclusions about the effective ingredients of psychological change and emotional growth.

In this book, Gerry Piaget and Barbara Binkley iden-
tify the main factors that create "barriers," habit patterns
that keep people from reaching their goals and cause
untold misery and frustration. In step-by-step sequences,
they describe a powerful set of tactics and methods for
overcoming these barriers. However, they go far beyond
techniques *per se,* and enter the more elegant domain of
personal appraisal, where the *intention to change within a
framework of self-acceptance* becomes all-important. In the
process, they underscore the fact that there are no panaceas, that nothing can take the place of diligent, repetitive
practice. Moreover, they emphasize the importance of
goal and problem specification, without which hazy ideas
only lead to hazy outcomes. Hence the need to define
goals, ferret out individual barrier patterns, and implement proven strategies that result in desired changes.
Their book spells out exactly how to attain these objec-
tives.

Unlike many books of this genre, *Overcoming Your
Barriers* remains sensitive to individual differences, to
personalistic variables. The cliché, "different strokes for
different folks," is one that many people echo only to then
write books that advocate universal truths and provide
nostrums for the whole of humankind. Piaget and Binkley
have studiously avoided falling into this trap. Indeed, a
person who grows strawberries for a living may be
tempted to proclaim that strawberries are good for everyone. He or she might accurately point out that strawberries are low in calories, high in potassium, and contain
calcium, phosphorus, and Vitamin A. So why shouldn't

everybody eat strawberries? For one thing, some people may dislike the fruit's taste and texture. Others may find that strawberries disagree with them—cause heartburn or indigestion. Some may be allergic to strawberries and can become deathly ill. And so it is with psychological procedures. Some people derive immense benefits from meditation, relaxation, or aerobic exercise. Others are exceedingly "allergic" to these practices. The authors of this book are well aware of the need to fit the right method to the right person, and bend over backwards to stress that the same tactical changes don't work for everyone.

Most traditional approaches tend to couch matters in terms that merely pathologize particular problems. The barriers concept is most useful in helping to specify the steps that need to be taken to remedy, rather than simply categorize, a behavioral or emotional problem. Here is a typical example from my own practice. A 32-year-old female executive was about to obtain an important promotion when she began suffering from insomnia, agitation, and depression. She consulted a therapist for several months who concluded that her problems emanated from an underlying fear of success, that she had an unconscious need to fail. She was in disagreement with this formulation and came to me for a second opinion. It seemed to me that this woman was genuinely interested in succeeding (I could detect no hidden needs of failure), but her fears and depressions were due to several interrelated factors: 1) She wasn't certain what her responsibilities would be in her new position, and what specific job skills might be called for. In her uncertainty she was constantly haunted by the fear that the Peter Principle had finally caught up with her. 2) She was exceedingly tense and had never been taught effective relaxation procedures. 3) She had images of failure and didn't know how to use her mind's eye to picture successes instead. 4) She was something of a perfectionist and held the viewpoint that her self-worth was almost entirely dependent on her work performance. 5) Her family, for reasons of its own, tended to put her down; although she was generally assertive at work, she lacked assertive skills with close family members.

Relaxation training, positive imagery work, and cognitive restructuring (as described in Chapter 8) effected a remarkable change within about six weeks. She found the courage to speak with her boss who convinced her that she had all the necessary abilities for the new position. Her most difficult task was to emancipate herself from her family. In this area, as in others, identifying precise goals and barriers aided her in achieving the changes she had come to therapy to make.

Many people do require professional help. If you are currently in or are seeking therapy—or are yourself a therapist on the lookout for better ways to serve your clients—this book will provide a most valuable treatment adjunct. In other instances, the procedures described here may help you make positive changes on your own and circumvent the need for outside assistance.

This is a rare book in that it describes methods of effective change in sufficient detail for readers to be able to apply them on a self-help basis. It makes important professional insights, skills, and wisdom available to the lay person. It provides immediate answers for anyone interested in overcoming his or her barriers and thereby coping more effectively with the challenges of daily living. If you are willing to work at it, this book can open important vistas for you.

Arnold A. Lazarus, Ph.D.
Professor, Graduate School of Applied and
Professional Psychology,
Rutgers University
Executive Director, Multimodal Therapy
Institutes

SECTION I

Exploring Your Barriers

1

Barriers to Change

Peter wants to succeed in the real estate business. Yet he chronically "forgets" to return phone calls, puts off going to work nearly every morning, and gets tighter than a banjo string at the least sign of rejection. Margaret wants to lose weight but can't seem to keep herself on a diet. Mary would like to be comfortable at social events and eventually become involved with a man. But she never goes to parties, and attractive strangers just about give her hives.

What is going on here? Why is it that Margaret eats chocolate cake while dreaming about getting her figure back? Why does Peter avoid calling a prospective client when flat rejection would leave him no poorer nor less successful than he is now? What keeps Mary in front of her television on Saturday evenings while loneliness and self-disgust nearly drive her mad? These people aren't hope-less depressives waiting for the first opportunity to do themselves in. They are "normal neurotics" like the rest of us: pleasure-seeking, pain-avoiding creatures who generally do their best to optimize their three-score-and-ten on this planet, and essentially believe in leading pleasant, meaningful lives.

So what stops them? In our terminology, their *barriers* stop them.

Barriers as Biocomputer Programs

In some ways human beings may be likened to com-plicated, mobile, programmable computers. The brain and body serve as the computer's "hardware." Experience provides the "software," as does that elusive construct we call the "mind." Sense organs are the input channels for entering data, while the body provides an array of output channels (vocal chords, hands, facial muscles, and so on) that can deliver information to the outside world in a variety of "languages."

When properly programmed, our biocomputers are of immense value to us; we literally couldn't get along without them. But they can also be easily misprogrammed and end up producing garbage—or worse. *Barrier systems* are the result of misprogramming—software that pro-duces undesirable outcomes.

Barrier systems are made up of highly complex sen-sory and behavior patterns. That is, they are composed of sequences of visual images, sound images, feelings, thoughts, and physical sensations woven together into memories, beliefs, habits, and other complex response patterns. Each *barrier element* (an individual image, sensation, etc.) in a particular sequence is triggered by one or more of the previous elements in the chain, and it in turn triggers off the element or elements following.

Barrier sequences (chains of barrier elements) often loop back on themselves and reconnect, forming closed *feedback loops* (self-triggering, never-ending patterns often called "vicious circles").

Here is a greatly simplified example of a barrier system. Our friend Margaret has had somewhat of a weight problem all her life. She's tried all the popular diets—well, more specifically she has read all the popular diet *books*. Beginning a diet/exercise program and sticking to one are very different issues for Margaret. But now she has a new book, *The Thirty-Day East Trenton Celery and Buffalo Chip Dieter's Handbook* (guaranteed satisfaction or your money cheerfully refunded), and she's determined.

On Monday morning Margaret sets her first objective: losing ten pounds in a month. So that evening, instead of heading for the chocolate cake, she gets out the Melba Toast and vaseline, carefully weighs her portion, pours a glass of low-calorie wine, and sits down to watch Star Trek reruns. But the feel of her TV chair (the location of much prior gorging) and the sight of a Klingon battleship remind her of the cake she usually eats after work. She's brought some tension from the office home with her, and thinks of how relaxing that rich food would taste sliding down. Quickly she says to herself, "You're on a diet, you fat slob!" She feels a flash of anger, a part of her pouts; "Why shouldn't I have just one piece? It isn't fair . . ." She tries to push that thought away and concentrate on Mr. Spock, but can't. "That cake . . . God, I'm hungry."

Then the phone rings. It's a wrong number, but it gets Margaret thinking about Stanley, who hasn't called since their first Friday night. Quick picture of Stanley with another woman, laughing. Suddenly Margaret feels alone, sad, and asks in a petulant voice, "Why bother? I can start this stupid diet tomorrow." She visualizes the cake, her mouth waters; somehow she can't get comfortable in the chair. At this point the TV station breaks for a commercial, and Margaret breaks for the refrigerator.

There is no question that an inner Margaret would honestly like to be thin. But complicated and well-practiced sequences of visual images, self-statements, feelings, behaviors, environmental cues, and random sensory stimuli are clearly leading her away from rather than toward any such goal. And the pattern by no means stops here. As Margaret returns to her chair with the cake she barrages herself with rationalizations intended to drive from her mind any final thoughts of Melba toast and mute the guilt feelings that are beginning to surface. "One little piece isn't going to hurt anything. . . . No one cares how I look anyway, why should I? . . . I guess I'm just weak-willed, I may as well accept it."

Then she eats the slice and it tastes fantastic, so during the next commercial she goes back and finishes the cake. (At least now that it's finished she doesn't have to sit around worrying about whether or not to eat it.) In spite of the self-recrimination she feels even as she licks the icing off her fork, eating the cake provides Margaret with safe, intense, and immediate gratification that soundly rewards all the behaviors and feelings we've described so far. That is, her actions reinforce her barrier system, those learned patterns of sensation and behavior that lead her away from the outcome she really believes she wants, and into a land where avoidance is King and Stanleys never roam.

If you think this is a bit exaggerated, talk to someone who has trouble dieting or is trying to control some other habit. We think we're understating our case, not over-stating it. We merely touched on but a few of the elements Margaret's biocomputer processed while she played Should-I-Or-Shouldn't-I with the cake. We don't mean to imply that she was *aware* of most of this; barrier systems function most effectively outside of conscious awareness.

Sometimes barrier systems are triggered by stressful events—that is, occurrences perceived to be potentially dangerous. This is often true of Peter, the real estate salesman. Peter's blood pressure is on the rise, so he is making a point of taking fifteen or twenty minutes each day before lunch to relax. One morning, he picks up the phone and hears a voice on the other end tell him that his income tax returns for last year have been chosen for audit. "That can't be!", he manages to gurgle. "I never got a letter in the mail."

"Must have been held up," comes the casual reply. "When would it be convenient for us to get together?"

Peter hangs up the phone, flops back into his chair, puts his head in his hands. He remembers all the opera tickets and family dinners he wrote off as business enter-tainment expenses. He visualizes the two St. Bernards he declared as dependents. He hears the voice of the auditor criticizing him, and his mind flashes back to a memory of the way his father used to stand over him, shaking his finger, when he was five or six. (He may not be conscious of this memory, but it's there.) He feels his mouth go dry and realizes that the back of his neck is beginning to ache, as it always does when he's under pressure. Peter says to himself, "Well, I'd better call a lawyer," and then feels his guts tighten as he imagines how much all of this is going to cost. But now the muscles across Peter's shoulders are like a rock. He rises from his desk and begins to pace.

The telephone call Peter received from his friendly IRS agent triggered a sequence of reaction patterns that we call a barrier system. The sequence may eventually lead him to stop work early because of a headache, become so frustrated that he bites his secretary's head off, or reach into his lower righthand desk drawer for that bottle of Johnny Walker Red two or three hours earlier in the afternoon than usual. But one place we guarantee it will *not* take him is to his original goal: relaxing for fifteen or twenty minutes before lunch.

Barrier Modalities

Ultimately all barrier systems can be broken down into sensory and behavioral elements—into see/hear/feel/taste/touch/do terms. However, the human mind/body (the biocomputer) also functions in a way that "sorts" stored experience into categories, or modes. These experience modalities help people deal more effectively with the mass of data they must process every day of their lives. During barrier analysis it often becomes expedient to work with *patterns* of experience, rather than *elements* of experience. Here are the eight modalities we use most frequently when working with a pattern level.

1. Memories

Biocomputers store sensory data for use later on.

"Remembering" involves accessing that data. What is important here, as far as our programming is concerned, is that recalled information has much the same effect as new information. For instance, when Peter unconsciously recalls an image of his father criticizing him, his body reacts as if his father were actually in the room. Often, the reaction won't be as strong as it was the first time; on the other hand, Peter may very well exaggerate in memory the intensity of his father's behavior and react even more strongly than he did the first time. The fact that much of this may be happening on an unconscious level is quite inconsequential—Peter's shoulders will get just as tense. Then, of course, he stores this memory as a new experience (which it is); later, he may remember it, as well as the original incident, when his boss yells at him. This "piling-on" effect can increase the power of a singly negative incident many-fold.

2. Anticipations

Most people are able to imagine things they've never experienced, or have experienced only vicariously. For instance, Peter is unsettled at the thought of an IRS audit. He's never been audited before, but the image of a large, critical man pointing a finger at him and asking him about his St. Bernards is still very real to him.

These types of anticipations, most important in barrier analysis, are called *worst-possible fantasies*. As the name implies, there are images that detail the absolute worst outcomes that could be associated with a particular situation. Peter, for example, imagines the horrors of tax court and the resulting prison sentence. Margaret imagines that no one will ever call her again, and that she will grow old, lonely and alone. Worst-possible fantasies tend to either inhibit the behavior in question (Mary chooses not to say hello to the attractive stranger) or lead to active avoidance maneuvers (Peter takes a good hit from the Johnny Walker bottle).

3. Feelings

When we talk of our "feelings," we are usually referring to a very complex pattern of sensations that we've learned to recognize and label. When Peter tells his wife that he feels "anxious" about the impending audit, he means that his stomach feels tense, his mouth is dry, he can't concentrate on his work, and the tips of his fingers are tender from all the nail-biting he's done over the past week. Similarly, feelings such as anger, sadness and excitement are not discrete sensory experiences, but rather patterns of awareness.

Feeling patterns can be most insidious when, in conjunction with behaviors, anticipations and other structures, they become self-rewarding feedback loops (vicious circles) within the barrier system. For example, the shy young man at the singles party feels nervous when an attractive woman smiles at him. So he drops his eyes, avoiding her gaze. Now, this doesn't do a whole lot for his chances with the lady, but looking elsewhere does help him feel more comfortable for the time being. Feeling better in turn rewards the looking-away behavior, even though in the long run the outcome is negative (no companionship that night). We'll discuss feedback loops in greater detail in the next section.

4. Behaviors

Nervous habits such as stuttering, blushing or talking too loudly are included here, as are a propensity for breaking eye contact under stress, drinking excessively or using a candy-flavored mouthwash. Sometimes very complex patterns can be broken down and identified. For instance, Meyer Friedman of Mt. Zion Hospital in San Francisco, has described patterns he calls "Type A behavior" which have been found to correlate with the incidence of coronary heart disease. Common Type A patterns include eating quickly, driving competitively in freeway traffic, setting rigid time schedules at work, talking in a sharp, staccato rhythm, and kicking the family dog.

The *absence* of certain behaviors may contribute to the power of a barrier system as well. For instance, not brushing one's teeth can be a barrier to a lot of things.

5. Thoughts and Cognitions

Thought processes can also loop back on themselves to form powerful barrier substructures. Ruminations and obsessions are extreme examples of this kind of mental loop. The graduate student who cannot get that sexy teaching assistant out of her mind may have some difficulty in performing up to expectations on her religious studies final. If Peter can't stop thinking about tax court, he isn't going to prepare for the audit very effectively, and his efficiency at the office may suffer as well. In addition, trying *not* to think can lead to paradoxical behavior patterns. The more Peter tries to get his mind off his tax troubles, the more difficult it becomes to think of anything else. As a trivial example of that, try not to think of

red alligators for the next five seconds. One . . . two . . .
three . . . four . . . five. How'd you do?

6. Self-Statements

There is a tremendous amount of power in what we
say to ourselves. The "power of positive thinking" is
well-known. The inhibiting, debilitating power of negative thinking should be equally so. Some psychologists
think people's entire self-concepts derive from what they
say to themselves. This is a little frightening, given that
most people are hardest on themselves just when they
most need a kind word and a little friendly support.
Remember the last time you made a significant mistake at
work and were caught at it. Did you say to yourself,
"Well, kid, you're OK. You blew that one, but you'll have
lots more chances to show your stuff!" If you did, we
would like to take your next workshop. Most people tend
to be more critical than the boss was. "You idiot, how
could you *do* that? You'll be fired, you know! Marge will
kill you! The kids will starve! And your *father* . . ."
Positive self-statements, when used to rationalize, avoid,
or excuse, can be equally negative. Remember Margaret?
Statements implying self-acceptance and the willingness
to be fair led her directly to the refrigerator and another
couple of pounds.

7. Semantic Patterns

The form as well as the content of verbal behavior can
contribute to the structure of a barrier system. The power
of labels provides a common example. Other things equal,
the individual who is referred to by friends and associates

as a "maintenance technician" probably feels better about herself and her job than the person who is simply called a janitor. Another common and powerful semantic form is called *implied cause*. As Johnny is driving home from work, he says to himself, "If Nancy loves me, she'll have dinner on the table when I get home!" Most of us will agree, at least in theory, that prompt dinner service and spousal love don't necessarily have very much to do with one another. Yet the form of Johnny's self-statement implies that they are closely related, that the absence of one proves the absence of the other. If he has convinced himself enough and comes home to find dinner unprepared, he may well spend the early evening feeling unloved as well as hungry.

8. Belief Systems

Beliefs are complex structures composed of visual, verbal and emotional elements that have somehow looped themselves into a self-reinforcing, curiously inflexible pattern. The presence of this feedback loop within the barrier system makes the structures very difficult to change from the outside. Beliefs themselves can be roughly subdivided into *values* (goods and bads, rights and wrongs, shoulds and shouldn'ts) and *viewpoints* (the shadings, biases and other unique perspectives that comprise a particular individual's world view). Belief systems can be valuable in that they create order and predictability in a confusing, often hostile world. On the other hand, they impose arbitrary rules and standards upon people, rules that serve no apparent long-term function other than to limit the boundaries of people's lives. In addition, belief systems have the curious characteristic of being *self-vali-*

dating. That is, they set out to prove themselves, and, to the believer, appear to succeed. Apparently, the data-processing filters imposed by a belief system lead our bio-computers to interpret objective data in a manner consistent with the belief system, ignoring all other interpretations. Using that approach, any data can be used to prove anything!

These eight categories—memories, anticipations, feelings, behaviors, thoughts, self-statements, semantic patterns and belief systems—are the ones we've found most helpful during barrier analysis. The categories overlap and may therefore provide us with different ways of looking at the same information.

Completing a "barrier mode survey" is the best way we know of finding the critical elements in barrier systems. The specific procedure that we use is outlined in Chapter 3. Another very comprehensive approach to the subject is described by Arnold Lazarus in *The Practice of Multimodal Therapy.* We are indebted to Dr. Lazarus for the contributions his ideas have made to our work, and we refer you to him for additional information.

Now we turn our attention to the mechanism by which barrier systems are maintained, reinforced and allowed to remain functioning: the avoidance loop.

Our story begins many years ago. . . .

The Avoidance Loop

Oog the Caveman had a realistic problem with pterodactyls. Every time Oog sensed the shadow of a pterodactyl in the sky, his sympathetic nervous system prepared him to fight or flee. Pterodactyl shadow—flash!

Off for the cave. Oog also learned easily to generalize (to assume that brown pterodactyls were just as dangerous as black ones) and to discriminate (to tell pterodactyl shadows from the shadows of pterodactyl-shaped clouds) so that he could spend more time outside the cave chasing eohippi and feeding his family.

Natural selection being what it is, modern man also uses fight-or-flight tactics for survival. (We assure you that none of us is descended from cave persons who did not learn to avoid pterodactyls.) And this is indisputably valuable when the situation involved contains a real, physical danger. There is nothing at all wrong with responding automatically to a rapidly approaching Doberman or to the rumbling shudder that may indicate an earthquake.

However, the dangers facing man in his modern society are usually different from those with which Oog had to deal. Singles bars, business meetings and income tax audits don't threaten our physical survival no matter how bad they get, and thus they don't call for retreat or physical attack. Most of us don't have much use for the fight-or-flight reaction anymore.

Yet, when the fellow who controls that lucrative account tells us that he's thinking of moving his business down the street, we become Oogs in business suits, with coursing adrenaline, tensing muscles and sweating palms. The long-term result, of course, is not survival at all; but rather, hypertension, a growing ulcer, and the possibility of eventual cardiovascular disease. And the avoidance behaviors and other barrier patterns we utilize in attempting to alleviate the situation only make matters worse.

Here is Mary, who feels desperately lonely but still spends her evenings watching television. Mary doesn't particularly like staying home on Saturday night, but she enjoys going alone to singles bars and parties a whole lot less. When she first thinks of going out, her anxiety increases, and if she continues to plan such an evening she becomes progressively more uncomfortable. She sees herself walking into Chuck's Cellar and imagines everyone turning to look at her as she enters. She feels tremendously out of place, and she knows that everyone else recognizes this. As she dresses, these worst-possible anticipations continue. She imagines being ignored or ridiculed all evening, stuttering whenever she tries to talk, being pawed by men, being snickered at by the "in crowd," and generally being played for a pathetic, aging fool.

Her fantasies work overtime, and at some point her anxiety level reaches an intensity that makes the prospect of staying at home alone again seem much the lesser of two evils. So she decides to forget the singles bar idea and watch television instead. That is, she chooses to avoid Chuck's Cellar in order to escape what she fears might happen there. As she does so, she immediately experiences a considerable amount of *anxiety-relief*.

Mary has spent the last couple of hours building up a twelve-cylinder anxiety reaction, and the reduction of that anxiety feels very positive indeed. That positive experience, following so closely on the heels of Mary's choice to stay home, has powerful reward properties. It doesn't matter that Mary will spend the balance of the evening hating herself for her cowardice and being depressed over her lack of companionship. The immediate gratification she receives by choosing to avoid the bar will serve to reinforce her tendency to avoid fearful situations and will increase the probability that she will choose TV over

Chuck's again next Saturday night. What's worse, Mary's aversion to singles bars will be rewarded and maintained as well. By thinking of going out Saturday night, becoming anxious, and then feeling relieved as a consequence of choosing to stay home, Mary is actually teaching herself both to avoid fearful experiences and to continue to fear them.

Psychologists call this pattern "avoidance learning." Essentially, a feedback loop is formed in the barrier system. With this loop installed, the program becomes self-rewarding and self-maintaining. Now Mary never has to go to a party or bar again let alone have a negative experience at one in order to remain frightened of the social scene for the rest of her days. All she must do is anticipate going to the bar or party clearly enough to raise her anxiety level, choose to stay home, and experience the anxiety-relief that accompanies the avoidance choice. This process of *negative reinforcement* (a good feeling caused by the reduction of a negative experience) can maintain her barrier system indefinitely with very little help from external sources.

Over time, these patterns become much more complex and begin to overlap. After a while, Mary won't know whether it is the men, the strangers, or the close quarters that frighten her most about Chuck's. In a rather forlorn attempt to retain a few shreds of self-esteem, she may begin to rationalize and defend the very barriers that are inhibiting her. She may develop semantic ploys ("I'm just a weak person—I couldn't resist."), irrational beliefs ("Everyone in a singles bar is plastic anyway."), and/or a legion of other strategies to help her bear the negative patterns she has been unable or unwilling to break. Unfortunately, these strategies will not help Mary feel better about herself in the long run. Mainly, they will only serve to reinforce and help perpetuate her problems.

Ultimately, barrier sequences become so entangled that they solidify into a lifestyle, a set of pre-programmed and counter-productive ruts. People become virtual robots, moving through rigid, narrow daily routines, fearing any changes, yet finding the thought of not changing unbearable . . . saying "yes" for fear of the consequences of saying "no" and "no" for fear of the consequences of saying "yes" . . . living in order to exist . . . being unhappy, and almost having forgotten why.

A poignant description of this existential dead-end appears in Castaneda's *Tales of Power*. Don Juan and Carlos are alone in the desert one night. They have just completed a very powerful experience together. Now, sitting quietly, they hear the barking of a lone dog coming from the direction of town. Don Juan tells Carlos that the dog is expressing the isolation and despair of its master; a man trapped in a life that he allows to control him, a life that has lost its excitement and meaning:

> "That barking and loneliness it creates speaks of the feelings of men," he went on. "Men for whom an entire life was like one Sunday afternoon which was not altogether, but rather hot and dull and uncomfortable. They sweated and fussed a great deal. They didn't know where to go or what to do. That afternoon left them only with the memory of petty annoyances and tedium, and then suddenly it was over, it was already night."

Responsibility and Blame

Let's return to Mary. This excerpt from her personal journal recounts one of the experiences that convinced her to seek professional help:

I tried to go into the party, but I couldn't. I sat there in my car for at least half an hour, getting colder and more frustrated every minute. Then, to keep warm, I drove around the block a few times. I really did want to go in—or part of me did, anyway—but as I drove, I could imagine walking up to the door and seeing all those strangers. Some of them would turn to stare at me . . . "I wonder who the old bag is?" I just couldn't face it. Then I thought of going back to the apartment, spending another evening alone, but I knew I couldn't face that either. I drove back to the party, parked a block away where I could find space, and got out of the car—but I couldn't make myself go any further. I was too self-conscious. I began to think of all kinds of reasons not to go, although at the same time I knew they were all bunk. I remember thinking, "What if it's the wrong house?" Crazy—I knew it was the right house: I could hear noises and music from where I stood. I leaned against the car for a few minutes, watching my breath and feeling perfectly miserable. Then, when another car parked down the street, I climbed back inside so the couple heading for the party couldn't see me. A few minutes later I drove home. I thought briefly of going to a movie instead, but it

was Saturday night, and I would have felt uncomfortable being seen there alone.

Consider what happened here. Mary didn't simply
"not go to a party." She spent an entire evening sitting in
her car, cold and miserable, trying to persuade herself to
take a "tremendous risk" that was mostly of her own
fabrication in the first place. Most of her attention was
directed into the future, riding the crest of worst-possible
fantasies that were all but totally unrealistic. In her frantic
search for a good excuse to go home, she tried to convince
herself that she had the wrong house despite indisputable
sensory evidence to the contrary. Then she actually hid
from a passing couple who were obviously bound for the
same party. In the face of her conflict, Mary exhibited an
extremely complex set of cognitive, emotional and overt
behaviors—irrational and, for all practical purposes,
completely outside her control.

We repeat: Mary had very little control over the
manner in which she behaved that evening. She thought
she should have had more control than she did, and later
berated herself roundly for her cowardice, even as she
turned on the television set and breathed a sigh of relief.
Self-criticism, based on the impression that she could have
done something other than what she did, led to feelings of
confusion, depression and self-doubt. These feelings became associated with her general reaction to parties and,
thus, ensured that the next time she would find attending
one even more difficult.

The whole issue of self-responsibility is tricky. On
the one hand, "humanists" tell us we are responsible for
our own behavior, even though we had little control over
the genetic and environmental forces that shaped it. On

the other hand, proponents of "determinism" tell us our behavior (and everything else, for that matter) has been determined that what will be will be, and we have very little to say about it. Mary, of course, deals herself the worst of both worlds: she blames herself for not choosing to attend parties, and then she acts like Roberta the Robot when she's invited to one.

We have no formal position on the determinism issue. Certainly it does no good to blame ourselves for pre-programmed patterns over which we have no control, of which, indeed, we are barely aware. Blame and guilt have powerful barrier properties of their own. Neither does it help to admonish ourselves to "take responsibility for what we've done." Mature, self-responsibility is to be valued—but all too often "responsibility" is simply a euphemism for "blame." (What did you really mean the last time you said, "Oh dear, I feel responsible for . . ."?)

In our clinical work, we suggest that people take a deterministic position about events in their lives that have *already occurred*. For instance, we would tell Mary that she'd been carefully trained to panic outside parties and that anyone with her genetic and environmental history would act as she did. In our model, her behavior is non-volitional and most emphatically not her fault. However, we suggest that people assume they do have choice when it comes to *future* occurrences. It is central to the philosophy of barrier analysis that Mary take complete responsibility for the manner in which she handles her *next* opportunity to attend a party. Having contacted us or having initiated barrier analysis on her own, she now knows where she is stuck. She now has an awareness and a knowledge of change tactics at her disposal that will help to reprogram her biocomputer and dissolve the barriers that keep her from attending parties. If she chooses to attend the parties, fine; if not, that's fine too. Either way, responsibility for making and implementing the choice is hers.*

SUMMARY

Barriers are patterns of stored sensory experience and behavioral responses that form sets of complex interlocking chains. Rather than stopping us in our tracks, these barrier patterns lead us away from our goals and into self-reinforcing, circular paths from which it can be singularly difficult to escape. *Barrier analysis* involves a series of processes in which barrier patterns are explored in depth, brought to conscious awareness, and then systematically remodeled.

This chapter has provided a brief and oversimplified view of some of the ways that barrier systems are developed and maintained. From an initial tendency to seek pleasure and avoid pain, we develop avoidance patterns that can inadvertently block the attainment of positive goals. To these avoidance patterns we add rationalizations, beliefs, defense mechanisms, and other complex patterns that serve to solidify the barrier system. Eventually our barriers expand to fill our lives, leaving us with a choice between a "safe" but trivial existence or a life full of conflict and stress.

---

*We admit that our position on the responsibility issue seems a bit contradictory. Is it reasonable to consider a particular behavior both determined *and* free? Maybe not. Still, the position is one that has precedence even in the physical realm. For instance, physicists treat photons either as waves or as particles, pretty much according to their fancy. In fact, photons behave both as waves *and* as particles. Nonsense, from a practical standpoint but the apparent contradiction doesn't bother quantum physicists a bit.

Throughout this book we will stress the *automatic, cyclical* nature of barrier patterns. Barriers create conflict, which in turn gives rise to barriers. Sometimes these patterns seem to be the product of rational thought; they may even seem to reflect freedom of choice. This is an illusion. Barrier systems are automatic programs that, whether we like it or not, have been installed in our biocomputers and, when triggered, *run us*. We don't like to think of ourselves as robots, but when our barrier programs are triggered, that is how we behave. This book is offered in the hope that some of the strategies it contains will help you learn to *reprogram* your automatic response patterns and regain control of your actions and your life.

2

Goal Specification

When we began conducting barrier workshops a few years ago we spent very little time on goal setting. We figured that most people already knew how to set specific, reasonable goals for themselves, so we moved quickly into the next stages of barrier analysis.

That particular tactic did not turn out to be one of our more brilliant time-savers. There we were, a day or so into our workshop, finding people working like beavers on barriers to goals they barely understood. It should be obvious that uncertainty regarding where one is going can substantially increase the difficulty of getting there. But in fact, people are often unclear about goals they are struggling to reach. Setting clear goals and keeping them clear in the face of stress is not nearly as easy as we first thought. Older, grayer and wiser now, we go to great lengths to emphasize the importance of goal specification. About 25% of our workshop time is spent in this area.

Desired Differences

Formally speaking, a goal is a hypothetical state or condition that is *different in a desirable way* from a perceived present state or condition. That is, your goals represent differences between the way things are now and the way you think you would like them to be at some point in the future.

For example, Terry wants to carve a perfect series of parallel turns on the west face of KT-22 at Squaw Valley. He shudders with embarrassment every time he thinks of those awkward and cowardly stem Christies he resorted to last year, and he has all sorts of fantasies about what it would be like to ski really well. He compares the way he skis now with images of the way he'd like to ski, experiences a decided preference for the latter, and decides to do something about it. That set of images now constitutes a *goal*.

Most of our goals initially evolve out of a dissatisfaction that we feel toward some present condition. For instance, our friend Margaret has decided she is going to stay away from cake and lose some weight. Why? Because she thinks she's too fat and believes her obesity to be responsible for the fact that she has no boyfriend. She visualizes a variety of positive experiences that she thinks she would have if she were thinner—and being thinner becomes her goal. (Note that whether or not Margaret is *really* too fat is largely irrelevant. We all know people who look like they could be slipped under doors, yet are constantly on diets in order to lose that extra nine ounces.) Margaret's subjective experience of obesity makes the goal of losing weight very real for her. Of course, whether or not losing the weight will help her achieve the specific result she imagines (such as a boyfriend), is quite another story.

Doing quality work at this stage of the game usually makes barrier analysis and reprogramming a lot easier. Actually, goal specification can have a powerful impact on reprogramming. Vagueness, confusion and ambivalence hold a lot of people back. Sometimes barriers can be dissolved simply by restating vague or amorphous goals into concrete, workable terms.

PROCEDURES

The process for goal specification is organized around the "rule of the five W's" from the world of journalism. First, state your goal in general terms. Then specify it according to those old standbys: WHO, WHAT, WHERE, WHEN, and HOW.

Goal specification is best done with pencil and paper. Write your work down until you know the procedures well enough to be able to specify your goals *automatically* under stress. Even then it is a good idea to record your work when the issues involved are important ones.

STEP 1: Define a general goal—something you would like to be able to do (or feel) or would like to be able to stop doing (or feeling).

Even when setting a general goal, be as clear and specific as you can. "I want to be happier" may be philosophically accurate, but it doesn't qualify as a practical, workable goal.

Make sure you set a goal for *yourself*, not for someone

else. Barrier analysis is a powerful strategy that can help
you get more of what you want out of life, but it won't help
you get other people to do what you want them to. "I want
my daughter to get better grades" is not an appropriate
goal for barrier analysis. If you find yourself setting a goal
that involves changing someone else, rephrase it to reflect
a related change in your behavior—e.g., "I want to learn
ways to help my daughter do better in school."

Finally, we suggest that you set reasonable goals for
yourself. The definition of "reasonable" may be somewhat arbitrary, but "I want to be rich before Tuesday" or
"I want this book to write itself" are certainly not reasonable goals. Some examples of reasonable goals are "I want
to stop smoking" or "I want to learn to keep my temper
when my father-in-law yells at me" or "I want to finish my
book by March 1st."

Steps 2-5 can be done in any order. Feel free to skip
around or to switch back and forth between steps if you
think it might help.

**STEP 2:   Ask yourself, "WHO will I need to deal with
in order to reach my goal?"**

The WHO should be a specific individual or a group
of individuals. If you want to learn to stand up to your
father-in-law, then the WHO would be your father-in-
law. If your goal is to learn to speak well in public, then the
WHO might be some specific audience that you'll have the
opportunity to address in the near future. If your goal
involves learning to deal with a certain class of people
(such as authority figures), then the WHO would be some
specific member of that class—e.g., your boss or the
policeman on the corner.

In some cases it may be appropriate to fantasize an ideal WHO during the first phases of barrier analysis. This technique is often useful in dealing with worst-possible fantasies involving someone you haven't met yet. For example, if you'd like to learn to initiate conversation with attractive strangers without dying of anxiety in the process, you might fantasize an ideal "attractive stranger" who would be particularly frightening to approach. Later on, when you begin to practice with real strangers, you can substitute the individual at hand for your fantasy stranger.

Often your specified goal will not contain a WHO. Technically, the WHO is the antagonist in your situation—for example, the salesperson to whom you must return a badly fitting garment. But sometimes, no one else but you is involved. When your goal involves learning to meditate or maintaining a diet, for instance, you may leave the WHO category blank. If you feel that some inanimate object is the antagonist, make that object the WHO. For example, Terry stands at the crest of KT-22 and mumbles to himself, "I'll get you this time, you bitch!" No question about it—Terry has a WHO. Terry's WHO, in this case, is the mountain he hopes to conquer.

Generally, we suggest that you not name yourself as the WHO. You're always involved in the goal situation, so naming yourself doesn't provide any useful or practical distinction. However, there is one major exception to this rule. If you have learned to use some kind of "parts model" (see Chapter 4), to help you define your goal, then you may very well wish to designate yourself as part of the WHO. For instance, John would like to be more comfortable with nudity, and he believes that a part of himself that he has labeled his "critical parent" keeps him from doing so. John would certainly be justified in making his "critical parent" the WHO during goal specification.

STEP 3:   Ask yourself, "WHAT will I specifically need to do in order to reach my goal?

The important thing here is to define your goal in terms of a single, elemental step—a specific behavior that you can carry out or learn to carry out. Tactics that are often useful in defining the WHAT are *simplification, sequencing,* and *positive restatement.*

Simplification. Complex goals usually call for several simultaneous change strategies. In such cases we suggest that you *simplify* the complex goal into several separate sub-goals and work on them one at a time. For example, Martha would like to respond to her husband's jealousy in a "positive manner." As stated, her goal is impossibly vague—so her first step should be to define the specific behaviors involved in "responding positively." These behaviors might include relaxing while he expresses his anger and resentment, communicating empathy with some sort of active listening technique, telling herself that the jealousy really reflects love rather than criticism and rejection, or expressing her own feelings openly in the face of the stress she feels. Since it would be difficult for Martha to practice all these new behaviors simultaneously, she would need to choose one and work on that, putting off the others until later. So her first WHAT might be, "[When my husband yells at me] I will communicate empathy and understanding by listening carefully, paraphrasing when appropriate, and letting him know that I do care about the way he feels."

Sequencing. Long-term goals that can be attained only

in several steps (e.g., "I want to become my company's personnel manager by the end of the year") should be *sequenced*—that is, the several steps should be executed in order. First, break the complex general goal down into several sub-goals. Then ask yourself, "Which step must I do first?" and use that first step as your specific WHAT. Each remaining sub-goal in the sequence is handled in a similar fashion. Once this is done, attaining the overall goal becomes much easier—so much so that people occasionally doubt the value of the process because it seems so easy.

For instance, Ralph decided to go back to graduate school after working successfully for several years as a carpenter. But whenever he thought about doing so, he became so anxious that he quickly put the matter out of his mind. Weeks turned into months, leaving Ralph no closer to graduate school.

It seems that Ralph was used to being a relatively big fish in an intellectually small and financially secure pond, and he was frightened at the prospect of being a small fish in a large, insecure one. He worried about not being able to support his family while in school, failing scholastically, and being too old for graduate school. When he talked of these concerns, he admitted that they were silly—but he was still no closer to returning to school than he had been almost a year before.

We helped Ralph sequence his long-term goal—returning to graduate school—into independent, chronological components. Then we asked him what his first step would be. A critical portion of the interview follows.

> *Q:* If you really decided to go to USF next year, what would you do first?

A: Well, first I would have to get accepted into the program.

Q: Specifically, how would you go about doing that?

A: I guess they would have to like my transcripts and letters of recommendation . . .

Q: Specifically, how would you go about finding out whether or not they did?

A: I would submit an application form, transcripts, and letters of recommendation.

Q: Fine. What would be your *first* step?

A: Hmmm . . . write to the USF Admissions Office for an application.

Q: You don't have the application forms yet?

A: No.

Again, some people doubt this process at first: it seems trivial. But getting the first (or next) step accomplished *is* progress. Not only does it get you closer to your first goal, but it seems to have a desensitizing effect as well.

It is curious how often some people avoid Step 1 of the sequence because they are afraid of latter steps. In such cases, both goal-setting and reprogramming essentially involve separating the steps and getting them done one at a time. For example, we often treat writer's block in this manner. We ask the person to sequence in detail the steps he or she would need to go through in order to have Chapter 12 done by June 1st. The person's first goal, then, would involve implementing Step 1. In Ralph's case, the WHAT was originally "going back to grad school"; after goal specification it became "writing to USF for application forms." Neither was his next step "going back to grad school": when the forms arrived, his WHAT became "filling out and returning the forms." Even his next WHAT wasn't "going back to grad school" it was providing three letters of recommendation." By the time Ralph's WHAT actually became "going back to grad school", he had already been accepted to the program and had been in telephone contact with his potential student advisor.

Positive Form. Finally, restate your goal in *positive form* if necessary. Refer to the general goal you set in Step 1. If you described a behavior you would like to *stop* doing, now state specifically what you intend to do *instead.* For instance, Randy has decided that he wants to stop drinking beer when he comes home from work. To specify WHAT, he must decide specifically how he intends to spend the time he formerly used for drinking beer. He may choose to behave exactly as before, substituting diet A&W Root Beer for the fattening, alcoholic kind. He may choose to jog a couple of miles after work. Or he may simply decide to meditate for 20 minutes in his back yard in order to provide himself with the relaxation he once got from the brew. Similarly, the after-dinner smoker may choose to focus on his or her breathing while sitting quietly, to chew on celery stalks, or to leave the table immediately and go out back where he can scream mournfully and kick trees instead of having his usual cigarette.

Again, your final WHAT must be stated in simple and absolutely practical terms that describe what you plan to *do* as well as what you plan to *stop* doing. As we mentioned earlier, reprogramming works best when the goals and barriers involved have been broken down into discrete and specific elements. So be willing to let go of your need to change all at once, and force yourself to break down those general goals into bite-sized chunks. You'll make faster, surer progress that way. To quote a poker player we know, "It's better to win the little ones that to lose the big ones."

STEP 4: Ask yourself, "Specifically WHEN and WHERE will I implement my goal?

WHERE and WHEN are usually easy to specify. The important thing is getting yourself to specify them. Procrastination may not be the biggest single barrier pattern in everyone's life, but for many of us it probably comes close. It is natural to avoid that which we find uncomfortable—and one of the simplest ways to avoid things is to put them off.

This is not to say that your WHEN must be specified in clock time. Do so if you can; many WHENs, however, are contingent upon the behavior of another individual or a particular opportunity presenting itself. It is appropriate, for example, to state, "I will be assertive with Joe the next time he criticizes me." For similar reasons, WHERE need not be specified in terms of a geographic location. "I will refuse dessert and relax, with my hands in my lap, *wherever* we eat tonight" is a fine WHERE statement.

Finally, make sure that the WHEN you specify will occur or has an excellent chance of occuring in the near future. It does little good to define a goal that you don't intend to implement until sometime next year.

STEP 5:   Ask yourself, "Specifically HOW do I want to experience reaching my goal? Specifically HOW (in sensory terms) will I know that I have reached my goal?

Of the various steps in goal specification, most people report that finding the HOW gives them most trouble and, when they have been successful, yields the greatest rewards as well. We suggest that you keep the following two points in mind while specifying the HOW:

1. *Do not confuse HOW with "How do I reach my goal?"* At this point you should be specifying goals, not trying to reach them. In goal specification, rather, HOW means, "HOW will my sense organs signal to me that I have reached my goal? What will I hear, see, or feel when I'm there? What sensory experiences will let me know that I've successfully implemented the specific behavior set forth in Step 3?"

2. *Do not confuse HOW with WHAT.* In our workshops these two categories are often confused. They do in fact overlap somewhat, but WHAT refers more to the behaviors involved in achieving a goal, whereas HOW refers to the sensory experiences that may be present while the WHAT is being performed successfully. For example, Brian's general goal is to be assertive in the face of his father's criticism. His final goal specification might look something like this:

WHO: Father

WHAT: I'll say, "Dad, when you talk to me about [whatever] like that, I feel criticized. I know you love me, but I feel hurt when you say those things." I'll say it in a relaxed, nondefensive tone of voice and keep my body relaxed while doing so.

WHEN: The next time he criticizes me.

WHERE: Wherever.

HOW: I'll feel confident that I'm taking my best shot at standing up for myself without hurting Dad's feelings. I'll hear the relaxed but assertive tone in my voice. I'll see him receive my message. I'll feel nervous, but I'll feel very good afterwards.

Notice that there is some overlap between HOW and WHAT. This overlap should cause you no real difficulty, though. In your own work, use WHAT to refer primarily to a specific goal-oriented behavior; use HOW to refer to sensory experiences that will signal that you have successfully reached your goal.

STEP 6: **Ask yourself, "Realistically speaking, do I possess all the major skills necessary to reach this goal?" If the answer is "no," acquiring these skills becomes your first goal. Return to Step 1 and proceed.**

Although not a part of goal specification *per se*, this step provides a valuable reality check. In the beginning of this chapter we mentioned setting "reasonable goals." Essentially, if you have set an unreasonable goal for yourself, you have made a sequencing error. If, for instance, your goal is to win a dance contest Friday night, but you don't know how to dance very well, you've probably skipped a step. We respectfully suggest that you go back and learn how to dance.

When dealing with such things as emotional reactions or communication problems, most people *do* have at least the minimal skills they need to reach goals they've set for themselves. It is usually a barrier, not a lack of skill, that holds people back. Nevertheless, skill training plays a vital part in many reprogramming procedures. When you do need a skill, be aware of that need and go get the training. Otherwise, you're only setting yourself up to lose.

STEP 7:   **Ask yourself, "Do I have other goals that conflict with this one?" If the answer is "yes," describe those other goals. Prioritize them, and return to Step 1 if necessary.**

Step 7 is also not part of goal specification *per se*, but it does serve as an additional reality check. At this point in barrier analysis, though, the question posed by Step 7 may be a little difficult to answer. For the time being, clarify your priorities as best you can, and then move on. Goal conflicts will be treated in some detail in the next chapter.

SAMPLE GOAL SPECIFICATION

Goal-setting seems to work best for most people when they use some kind of self-interview format. Cycle through Steps 1-7 several times until you're satisfied that the goal you've selected has been whittled down to a workable level. The best way to do that is to check or question each response you've made and make sure that all experiences (such as "happiness") have been described in sensory terms and that all behavior patterns (such as "assertiveness") have been broken down into specific procedural steps.

There are a variety of self-interview styles that work well in goal specification. In our workshops we demonstrate our favorite styles with volunteers in front of the group before asking participants to complete their worksheets on their own. The following interview has been transcribed, with modifications, from one such workshop demonstration. As you read it, pay careful attention to the questions that we use to help Mary (whom you met in the last chapter) specify generalities and remain on the right track. Also note that the interviewer didn't follow any particular format, but rather skipped around from step to step as deemed appropriate. Advanced techniques of goal specification are difficult to learn from a book. Perhaps this example, however, will give you some idea of the ways in which the basic procedures can be employed. The right-hand column in the example provides a commentary on Mary's work.

Goal Specification: Visiting Parents

Q1: What's your goal, Mary?

A1: My parents are coming for the holidays. I'm glad they're coming—I'd hate to spend Christmas alone—but it's going to be hard. My mother comes right in and takes over. I feel they invade my privacy sometimes. And they're going to ask me why I'm not dating anyone . . .

A1: Mary responds to the initial question with a variety of fears and anticipations rather than with a goal.

Q2: Sounds like you're head-

ing for a merry Christmas.
What's your goal?

A2: I'd like to stand up to them for a change—especially my mother.

A2: "I'd like to stand up to my mother" constitutes a good general goal. The interviewer will now help Mary specify that goal according to the rule of the five W's.

Q3: How, specifically?

A3: Lots of ways. I've never told them how I really feel without just blowing up and screaming at them.

A3: Mary describes how she doesn't want to behave while standing up to her mother.

Q4: So you'd like to stand up to them without losing your temper . . .

A4: That would be wonderful, but I don't think I could do it. There are so many little things they . . .

Q5: Pick one.

Q5: When dealing with a complex issue like a relationship with a parent, it's important that you pick one specific element and start there. Don't get lost worrying about all the hundreds of places you could start.

A5: (She thinks.) My mother is going to ask me if my social life has improved, and when I say "no," she'll give me a cer-

A5: Note that Mary has answered the question "WHEN" with very specific sensory information.

tain look she has, half smug
and half sympathy . . . she'll
shrug and say something a-
bout my age . . . I *hate* that . . .

Q6: Specifically what would
you like to say or do the next
time she acts that way?

Q6: Specify "WHAT." That
is, what does Mary mean by
"stand up to Mother?"

A6: Tell her I don't like it. I
don't know—I could never
say that. I know! I'd like to use
that "I have a problem" technique you demonstrated yes-
terday.★

Q7: Specifically what will you
say?

Q7: When you goal is interpersonal, "WHAT" nearly always includes a specific statement you wish to make to the
other person.

A7: I'll say, "Mom, I have a
problem. I want to tell you
how upset I get when you imply that I'm turning into an
old maid, but I don't know
how I could do it without

A7: A good application of the
"I have a problem" tech-
nique.

★Use the "I have a problem" technique when a negative anticipation has been stopping
you from communicating with someone. Technically, this involves sending a "content
level" and a "process level" message simultaneously. Practially speaking, you ask for
help in a way that also gets your message across. For instance, Peter says to his father,
"Dad, I have a problem. I don't know how to tell you without making you angry that I
got married last night. Please help me." Peter's intent is to (1) communicate honest
concern about Dad's feelings, and (2) get Dad on Peter's side *before* the anticipated
blowup can occur. While rarely totally successful, the "I have a problem" technique
often *helps* to partially defuse an emotionally loaded exchange.

hurting   your   feelings."
Should I bring it up, do you
think?

Q8: Beautiful! Mary, where
and when will you say this?

A8: The very next time Mom
starts in about my dating.
Probably in the car coming
home from the airport.

Q9: Specifically what do you
want to be doing while you're
talking to her?

A9: Not driving off the road in
hysteria! (Laughs.) I would
like to be calm and relaxed . . .
sound like a woman rather
than a whiny little girl . . . not
cry.

Q10: Would you be willing to
be adult and calm and re-
laxed—and also let yourself
cry if you had to? Just as a first
approximation?

Q10: It's permissible to set a
goal that involves not crying in
a particular situation. But
often it's not necessary. Crying doesn't get in a person's
way as much as they think it
does and since crying is a
natural expression of feeling,
it is sometimes difficult to reprogram. Here the interviewer thinks Mary will be able to
reach her goal more quickly—
be able to "stand up to her
mother"—if she allows herself
to cry while doing so.

A10: I guess so . . .

Q11: You see, I don't think you can choose not to cry—or even that you would want to, really. Crying is fine when you feel upset. But what if you could either let it out and cry with real gusto, like a strong, mature female human being, or try to hold it in and begin to whine . . .

A11: Yeah, I guess holding back does come out sort of whiney. OK, I'll either be dry-eyed or a real gusher!

Q12: Good! Now, how will you know that you've reached this specific goal?

Q12: An important question in goal specification. What will Mary see, hear and feel that will mean she's reached her goal and successfully stood up to her mother?

A12: I guess I'll hear myself say the words (or bawl!) . . . I'll feel relaxed . . . No— there's a certain feeling I'd have, a quiet kind of excitement and pride . . .

Q13: Specifically how would you know you had that feeling? What sensations . . . ?

A13: I can't explain it, but I'd know it!

A13: Sometimes it's difficult to describe certain feelings in sensory terms. It's not really necessary that you put all your feelings into words in order to goal-specify. But make sure that you do have specific, recognizable experiences in mind, whether you can articulate them precisely or not.

Q14: OK, fine. Specifically what might you see or hear?

A14: (Smiles.) I'd see a very surprised mother sitting over there! Oh, but then she'd get angry and turn away . . . I'd feel terrible, and . . .

A14: Mary begins to anticipate what would stop her from standing up to her mother. Mary's reactions to her mother's anger are not a part of this goal specification process! Another specific goal might be set in that regard— but remember, do one thing at a time.

Q15: Wait a minute—we'll get into your barriers later. If you stood up to your mother with the "I have a problem," technique, you'd feel a quiet pride, see a surprised look on her face, then maybe see and hear her get angry and look away?

Q15: The anger and looking away are reframed as indicators of success.

A15: Uh-huh.

A15: Mary would love to set the following goal: "I want to stand up to my mother without making her mad." But if she did so, Mary would actually be setting a goal for someone else (her mother). Specifying a goal that is contingent upon the cooperation of another person is not an effective change strategy and is in no way a part of this model. As far as we're concerned, it's the best way to set yourself up to lose. Set goals that relate to *your* own feelings and behavior.

Q16: OK, those signals would tell you that you'd successfully reached your goal. Mary, look. You're so primed to interpret any anger from your mother as negative! If you say what we've planned here and your mother gets annoyed, that's her business! You've done nothing wrong! You requested her help with a tricky issue and told her you were concerned about her feelings. Mary, if she gets mad at that it will be a positive sign for you! It will mean that you stood up to your mother in a polite, caring manner at a time when she probably was playing a little game—and knew it!

Q16: Again, at some point Mary may choose to set a goal involving learning to deal with her mother's feelings. But that goal specification process should be kept separate from this one, and the two issues (standing up to Mother and dealing with Mother's anger) should be seen and dealt with separately.

(At this point the interviewer moved on to discuss the conflicts Mary felt about confronting her parents, and initiated Parts Analysis (Chapter 4). Before ending the demonstration, Mary restated her specific goal.)

GENERAL GOAL:

I want to stand up to my parents during their holiday visit.

SPECIFIC GOAL:

WHO: Mother

WHAT: Use the "I have a problem" technique to share upset feelings in a relatively safe, empathetic fashion.

WHEN: When Mother forces a discussion of my social life (or other personal business that I would prefer not to discuss).

WHERE: Wherever it comes up (if there is a reasonable amount of privacy).

HOW: Relaxed, calm manner. Assertive body posture. Crying, if necessary; I will not choke tears in a whine. I will feel a quiet pride and may see/hear surprise and/or anger in Mother.

Setting Content-Free Goals

Our workshop participants occasionally express concern over the emphasis we place on goal specification. Some individuals who have had exposure to Eastern philosophy and thought believe that there is great spiritual and practical value in giving up any orientation toward goals. They would prefer simply letting go, flowing with the karma and letting be whatever may be. These people see in our work an overemphasis on structure and control and accuse us of ignoring the permissive, yielding Yin side of the human condition.

Yet we feel that our work has been profoundly affected by Eastern thought, in particular by the principles taught in Aikido and other martial arts. We strongly believe in the balance of Yin and Yang, in a blending of Eastern and Western ways. And we emphatically believe in the importance of being able to forsake goal-directed behavior and goal-oriented consciousness in order to simply "be." In fact, we sometimes help people specify and achieve the goal of giving up goals.

What we're talking about is the setting of *content-free goals*. When you set a content-free goal, your goal is to yield to or give into a particular experience—to follow rather than lead. The Aikido master has such a goal in mind when he enters into combat. Paying careful attention to the movement and energy patterns of his antagonist, he blends with, follows, virtually becomes one with those energies in order to eventually control them. He might then choose to throw his opponent to the mat. However, if the vagaries of leverage, chance and skill are such that his opponent is in a position to do the throwing, the Aikido master will immediately *choose to be thrown*. He yields; his goal becomes being thrown perfectly. By flowing with his opponent's energies, he maximizes the possibility of landing in a position from which he can take control and initiate a maneuver himself.

Thus, the Aikido master chooses to follow in order to lead. His goal is truly content-free: he has no way of knowing what will happen from one minute to the next. He simply allows the moment to dictate his moves. Yet few would claim that, while on the Aikido mat, he is not a most goal-directed fellow.

There are many such examples of content-free goals. Some we accept as commonplace: consider, for instance, the dancer whose goal is to follow his partner perfectly in a waltz or foxtrot. On the other hand, many examples seem paradoxical at first glance. One of the best ways to deal with insomnia, for example, is to try to stay awake all night.

It is impossible for anyone to be completely goal-free all the time. Perhaps it's impossible at any time. Particularly in Western culture, our civilization requires us to set and achieve certain goals in order to survive. Within that context, however, we may desire that certain of our goals be content-free, and if we are skillful we can learn to achieve these goals as well. We can do so because our minds can operate simultaneously on two logical levels of reality. Take, for instance, the formal meditator. On one level she is irreversibly goal-directed: she chooses that, for the next twenty minutes, she will have no goals at all and will simply experience the here-and-now. So she goes to a quiet part of her $200,000 house, closes the door, unrolls the straw mat she bought at Sears, assumes the lotus position and closes her eyes. She then experiences twenty minutes of relaxing, meditative, goal-free here-and-now, *all within a highly structured environment that she intentionally created through the achievement of a wide variety of very pragmatic goals.*

Goals only run your life if you think you need to reach them. Otherwise, they simply illuminate alternative pathways to a richer experience of living. So learn and practice the techniques of goal specification in the variety of ways in which they can be used; then you'll be free to explore those pathways that seem to have promise for you and ignore the rest—as you choose.

SUMMARY

A goal is a hypothetical state or condition that contains a desired difference from a real or imagined present state. Since most people find it easier to gripe about what they don't have and don't want than to specify exactly what they *do* want—and because setting specific goals is often threatening—we often leave our goals vague. Unfortunately, vague and general goals are a lot more difficult to achieve than clear, specific ones. Goal specification provides a practical method of breaking down ambiguous goals into specific components that can be handled individually. Doing so is the first concrete step in barrier analysis, but sometimes functions by itself as a powerful reprogramming tool. Practice specifying goals frequently, and you will become more proficient. Eventually you'll begin to specify "desired differences" automatically, and goal-setting will become just another part of the way in which you deal with the world. As your strategies for identifying and dealing with goals improve, so, too, (we believe) will the general quality of your life.

3

Barrier Analysis

The next step in our reprogramming format is barrier analysis. Here we'll try to find out exactly *what stops you* from reaching the goals you've set. As with goal-setting, emphasis is placed on the importance of specification. A detailed barrier analysis is half, and sometimes all, the battle. Once you can define the specific elements and patterns that are hanging you up, erasing or modifying them often poses little problem. Your biggest challenge here usually involves developing awareness. Most of us spend a good deal of time trying *not* to be aware of the characteristics that keep us (or allow us to remain) stuck.

Barrier specification is not always a pleasant task. It's one thing to set a goal and intend to reach it, and quite another to come face to face with the array of bad habits, memory patterns, fears, beliefs, rationalizations, and random psychological flotsam that immediately rise to block your path. It is amazing how the simplest, most straight-forward goals can interconnect with so many barrier components at once.

For instance, Jim is asked to make a presentation before ten or fifteen people at a company business meeting. He has learned to fear public speaking and to avoid it whenever he can. However, circumstances at work being what they are, he knows that this time he is going to have to perform.

Immediately his barrier programs go to work. A frightened, self-critical part of Jim begins to regurgitate negative self-statements: "I know I'm going to sound like a fool. The boss will finally get an idea of how incompetent I really am. What if I can't think of anything to say?" and so on. Simultaneously, he recalls himself as a fourth-grader giving an oral report on dinosaurs. He forgets his speech and is teased and ridiculed by his classmates. (Jim has carried that particular experience around with him for a long time; it is always there to serve him when his fear of public speaking needs a little energizing.) In addition, as he anticipates speaking at the business meeting, he recognizes another well-known reaction: his throat begins to get tight. Jim believes that when his throat feels tight he can't speak in public without sounding like a frog. He hates that image—he feels it makes him seem like a coward.

None of these reactions will help him much as he prepares and presents his speech. Indeed, they increase the likelihood that his day will progress just about the way he's afraid it will. Jim's barrier programs are such that they may eventually lead him into that most frustrating of situations: the self-fulfilling prophecy. Unless something is done to change things, he may very well spend the next few decades *trying* to sound relaxed and confident in front of groups—while succeeding only in proving to himself that he is a cowardly failure who should give up his podium for a lily pad on Walden Pond. Which brings us to the Try-Harder Fallacy.

The Try-Harder Fallacy

When it comes to dealing with situations like Jim's, most of us demonstrate a curious tendency. We try to solve our problem in one way or another, and then step back to see how we did. If our strategy worked and the problem is gone, great! But if it didn't work, we will *take the same solution and try harder with it,* rather than stop to look for a different and possibly more effective approach. This inflexibility limits the number of choices we can make regarding how to solve the problem at hand.

Sometimes the try-harder method works. Certainly it's been pounded into us from the cradle—not only by our parents and teachers, but by clichés and idioms that reflect the very fabric of our culture. "If at first you don't succeed, try, try again!" "Keep your nose to the grindstone."* And so on. Unfortunately, folk wisdom doesn't hold up very well in this case. More often than not, trying harder with an ineffective strategy actually helps to maintain or increase problems rather than solve them.

The negative effects of trying harder are all around us. Our friend Jim will *try* to relax (itself a contradiction in terms!) and *try* not to sound too much like a frog. Eventually he may try himself right into a full-bore public-speak-

---

*In *Winning Through Intimidation*, Robert J. Ringer mentions in passing that, he who keeps his nose to the grindstone usually winds up with a very short, very tender nose.

ing phobia. Similarly, Roger yells at his son for some reason; his son ignores him in favor of "The A Team" on TV. So of course, Roger yells louder. His son turns up the TV. Similarly, the fifty-dollar date didn't impress Marcia, who has simple tastes and doesn't much like Stanley anyway. But Stanley thinks he knows what to do next time out: he'll spend a hundred and fifty.

We'll discuss the Try-Harder Fallacy again later on (see Chapter 8). For now, keep in mind that trying harder can be a major barrier pattern leading to frustrating vicious circles and self-fulfilling prophecies. *Barrier analysis is intended to provide you with an alternative to trying harder*. Instead of trying to change, you pay careful attention to the patterns that are holding you back. Rather than struggling with a difficult problem, you begin instead to unravel the patterns and elements that may be keeping you from solving it. This, in turn, will increase the number of problem solving options available to you at a given point in time.

PROCEDURES

As before, we will first present the barrier analysis process in sequential steps, and then provide an annotated illustration from one of our workshops. However, the order in which you do Steps 4-8 is arbitrary. In practice you'll find yourself starting anywhere and then jumping around. We generally prefer to begin at the sensory level (What do you see/hear/feel that stops you?) and then move to larger, more abstract patterns from there. You may discover other starting points that work better for you.

STEP 1:   Restate a goal as in Chapter 2.

Restate your general goal, and then your specific goal in who/what/where/when/how form. If you've not yet adequately specified a goal before reading this chapter, go back to Chapter 2 and do so at this time.

STEP 2: Close your eyes. Focus inward. Clearly imagine trying to reach your goal. Describe what stops you from reaching it in general terms.

Your answers should be general at this step. But try to find all the major patterns that stop you from reaching your goal.

Imagine moving toward your goal. Each time you run into a barrier, describe it, and then, acting as if it were not there, continue moving toward your goal, looking for additional barrier patterns.

If you run into trouble, it may be because your goal is still too complicated, or hasn't been properly sequenced. If that's so, whittle it down to a workable size.

STEP 3: Define or locate the "part(s)" of you responsible for creating and maintaining your barrier system. Work with these parts when appropriate. Utilize their talents, insights, and unique viewpoints to help you complete an accurate barrier analysis.

Sometimes working with what we call the "Inner Family Model" can help clarify barrier elements and sequences.* According to this model, the "self" may be

---

*We extend our thanks here to Errol D. Schubot, Ph.D., who introduced us to inner family processing. Errol is truly a magician. His spells and incantations have greatly influenced our personal lives as well as the contents of this book.

divided into several parts, or subselves, which interact together as a kind of family and which represent different priorities and conflicting points of view.* These subselves may then be invited to communicate with one another. Various techniques can be used to help the process along and to aid in the development, clarification, and expression of your different parts. This procedure allows you to discuss your ambivalences and conflicts among yourselves (so to speak) and eventually reach compromises and/or deeper levels of self-awareness. Powerful retraining strategies may then be used to help your subselves learn to cooperate in setting and reaching goals.

Returning to our earlier example, we asked Jim to close his eyes and imagine the part of himself responsible for his fear of public speaking. After some discussion, Jim described the part as a lonely, easily-intimidated eight- or nine-year-old boy who was particularly frightened of being criticized for mistakes or failure. We suggested that Jim act as if this Frightened-Child part really existed, as a sort of internal younger brother. We further suggested that he and his Frightened Child work together as a team —literally have conversations with one another during barrier analysis, to define accurate, meaningful barrier patterns. At certain points we had Jim role-play his younger self, so that we could question the child directly. Later, as a reprogramming strategy, we asked him to imagine going back in time as his adult self to comfort and support the frightened nine-year-old. He wound up teach-

---

*A variety of contemporary psychotherapies use inner family work in one form or another. The most popular of these is Transactional Analysis, which emphasizes the use of three subselves: Parent, Adult, and Child.

ing his Frightened Child some of the assertion strategies he'd learned in our workshops.

Many of our students find that some of the barrier patterns they uncover are *part-specific*. That is, a problem memory, habit, belief, or other barrier component may best be attributed to one of your inner family members, rather than to "you" as a whole. When one of your parts appears to be holding you back, inner family work can greatly enhance the power of barrier analysis. In this case, a kind of second-order barrier analysis could be performed on/by the subself involved, with you and your other inner family members observing and/or helping out. A variation on this theme is described later in the chapter, when Ann has her Dead-Father part assist in a barrier analysis.

Using the Inner Family Model at this stage is optional; do so if you think it is appropriate or if nothing else seems to be working. In the next chapter we'll explore various applications of this model in greater depth, when we deal with motivation strategies and conflict resolution. In particular we'll describe some ways you can practice locating, defining, and communicating with valuable members of your own inner family.

STEP 4: **Break down your general barrier patterns into specific sensory experiences. What do you *see*, *hear*, and *feel*, as you imagine moving toward your goal, that might stop you? List as many of these specific barrier elements as you can.**

As mentioned earlier, the barrier patterns that stop us from seeking our goals are constructed of sequences of specific sensory elements. As Terry skis toward the mogul on which he intends to turn, he feels his legs tense, sees (in his mind's eye) the steepness of the slope beyond the mogul, feels himself stiffen and straighten his downhill leg as he completes his turn, feels himself leaning back on his skiis and into the hill, sees the reassuring closeness of the snow as he twists away from the fall-line . . . and all this happens in his mind as he approaches the mogul and prepares to turn. The outcome, of course, is an unavoidable fall on his behind.

As in Step 2, it will be necessary for you to imagine approaching your goal several times. Each time you run through the scene you will find additional sensory elements. Some of the ones you miss the first time around may be important, so be willing to spend a few extra moments on this step. Continue to imagine trying to reach your goal. Allow your sense of "what stops you" to expand and deepen. Specifically, what do you see, hear, and feel that might stop you? Compare the information you receive in each of these sensory modes. How does what you see relate to what you feel; how does what you feel relate to what you hear? and so on. What else do you see/hear/feel that might be keeping you back?

STEP 5:   Continue to focus inward. Allow your awareness to extend into the past and into the future. Ask yourself, "What experiences do I *remember* that might stop me from reaching my goal?" Then ask, "What outcomes do I *anticipate* that might stop me?"

Record any past images or old memories that attempting to reach your goal may bring to mind. Our barriers are derived in a large part from negative past experiences—from failures, rejections, and the like—which happened to us once and we anticipate may happen again. Such was Mary's experience, when she recalled what her mother said happened to "bad girls."

Sometimes, however, these memories seem to have no rational relationship to the goal in question. They are obviously connected emotionally, but for no logical reason. We once worked with a woman we'll call Martha who was deathly afraid of flying. For the final stages of her therapy, we convinced her to fly with us from San Francisco to Los Angeles. During the flight, we used a variety of reprogramming procedures (see Chapter 6) to help her become less sensitive to the experience of being in an airplane 31,000 feet over the Big Sur coastline.

Unfortunately the work didn't seem to be progressing very well. Twenty minutes into the flight Martha was still so frightened that she was barely able to concentrate on our instructions, let alone commit herself to carrying them out. Then, for no apparent reason, she vividly recalled a childhood experience involving the death of her cat. After working for a few minutes with that memory, Martha began to experience a dramatic shift in her reaction to flying. She found herself much more willing and able to concentrate on reprogramming procedures, and by the time our plane landed in Los Angeles her fear of flying had virtually disappeared. We had a cup of coffee, and then returned to San Jose; the second flight caused her only moderate distress, which continued to diminish as we worked.

So it doesn't matter whether or not the memories you access seem to have any direct relevance to the specific goal you're trying to reach. Write them down anyway. Then break them down into sensory terms, as you did in Step 3.

Next, record what you anticipate may happen if you try to attain your goal. Be especially aware of what we call "worst-possible" fantasies. These are images that, rationally, you're almost certain won't come true—but which, irrationally, are so frightening, depressing, or otherwise nauseous that hold you back anyway.

We all visualize worst-possible fantasies. Herbert, a civil servant for the County Health Department, wants to ask his boss for a special assignment. He knows his job is secure, and his boss has told him that he's considered a valuable employee at the hospital. Yet Herbert spends weeks agonizing over whether or not to make his request. Rationally, he knows the worst his boss can do is say no. But knowing that doesn't seem to help much. He visualizes the man looking at him in disgust, and in a voice dripping with scorn, saying, "Herbert, you poor little slob! I always knew you were a worthless, stupid drip with no understanding of your duties here. This proves it. Wait till the rest of the office finds out about this!"

Herbert probably isn't conscious of most of this process as it's happening. At the time, he only knows that when he thinks of making his request his stomach knots up and he somehow can't make himself knock on the boss' door. But through barrier analysis he may be able to discover more of what's really going on inside him—and therefore be in a much better position to do something about it.

Worst-possible fantasies are usually derived from memories of prior upsets or failures that have been distorted, exaggerated, generalized, and then projected into the future. When Lester asked the prettiest girl in his sophomore class to accompany him to the annual Artichoke Hop, she laughed and said, "Oh, I've already got a date," and walked away. But Lester took this refusal very seriously. He ruminated all weekend, and by Monday morning was so ashamed at the way the entire school had seen him ridiculed that he could barely make it to class. Now, a year later, Lester sweats buckets and goes through weeks of torture before getting up the nerve to ask someone for a date. Rationally, he knows he shouldn't be worried; most of the girls he did finally ask out during the year accepted. Further, he knows that if he does get turned down he won't be any worse off than he is now: still dateless for the weekend. But when he imagines walking up to a girl and popping the question, "worst-possibles" begin to flow like water. He sees the disgusted look on her face; he hears her laughter and the cruel mockery in her voice as she yells, "Hey, look at the nerd who just asked me out!" Lester feels like he's suddenly been transported into the middle of an E. F. Hutton commercial: people for a quarter-of-a-mile around freezing in their tracks and paying attention only to him; "When Lester gets dumped on, people listen!" Les may not be aware of all this consciously. But his body reacts to it nonetheless. His mouth goes dry, his mind goes blank, and his resolve to ask for a date goes down the tubes.

Again, try to record your anticipations in sensory terms: What do you imagine you will see, hear, and feel— and how do you feel now as a result that may keep you from reaching your goal?

STEP 6: Continue to move toward your goal in the face of the various experiences you described above. Now ask yourself: "What might I say to myself that would stop me?" Then ask, "What might I do that would stop me?"

You may have done some of this work already, during the last step. Memories and anticipations are often composed of and/or accompanied by self-statements and/or behaviors. Actually, anticipations and self-statements belong to the same category. They both may be considered internal "images." Certainly they perform many of the same functions. even so, making the distinction sometimes leads people to explore the same information from different angles, and wind up with a more thorough barrier analysis. At any rate, record whatever internal verbiage you think might be keeping you stuck.

Terry sees the slope falling off between his ski tips for what seems like miles. He stiffens his body as he groans, "I'll never be able to ski this sucker! I'll break every bone in my body!"

Judy thinks of how much bigger and more important the *San Francisco Examiner* is than her own small-town tabloid, and grumbles to herself, "I must be an idiot to think they'd accept my story."

As he watches the tennis ball slicing toward his backhand, Paul tells himself angrily, "Now don't tense up this time, don't tense up!" Of course he immediately tenses up and chops awkwardly at the ball. "Damn it, I *knew* I couldn't make that backhand shot!"

Sometimes the semantic structure as well as the content of a self-statement can cause trouble. (See Chapter 8.) For instance, an implied causative is a statement which implies that one condition or situation has caused another condition or situation to occur. Here's an example.

Stuck for half an hour in traffic, Randy grumbles to himself, "If she really cares about me, she'll have dinner ready when I get home." He's hungry, and tired, and feeling a little insecure because his boss criticized him that afternoon and he'd been afraid to speak up in his own defense. He remembers that his mother always had dinner ready for his father by the time he got home (forgetting that his mother didn't work herself); and he has seen what that "women's lib garbage" has done to the marriages of a couple of his friends. Anyway, he repeats the "if she loved me . . ." line to himself thirty or forty times during his long commute. He reaches home and finds a note saying that his wife has gone to the market and would like to go out to dinner that evening. Randy doesn't feel particularly angry—he knows his wife had to do the shopping—but somehow as he grabs a beer and sits down to watch the news, he feels just a little less . . . loved than he did before. The statements he muttered on the way home have taken their toll.

If you can bear to leave Randy at a time like this, take a moment to consider the behavior patterns that may be keeping you from your goal. Habits, idiosyncracies, mannerisms, and the like. Stammering, excessive drinking, fits of temper, and using the wrong mouthwash all qualify as behavioral barrier components. Write them down.

STEP 7: **Ask yourself, "What do I believe might stop**

me from reaching my goal? Specifically, what values might stop me? What biased or subjective points of view might stop me?

Values involve such issues as good and bad, right and wrong, should and shouldn't, innocence and guilt, and so on. Viewpoints, on the other hand, reflect the manner in which we organize our experience of the world around us. Thus, if John doesn't believe that flying saucers exist, he has a viewpoint; if he thinks flying saucers are *bad*, he has a value. If Jerry believes that Danielle makes him angry, that's a viewpoint. Believing that she was wrong to do so would be a value. Viewpoints help us organize and catalog our experiences; values help us score them.

Most beliefs, of course, contain both components. When Greta plops down in her therapist's chair and says, "I've got a problem with men," no doubt she is expressing both a value and a viewpoint. Issues having to do with problem definition, morality, ethics, and the like usually involve a great many values and viewpoints simultaneously.

Beliefs are more abstract than the other barrier elements we've discussed so far. What we see, hear, feel, remember, anticipate, and say to ourselves all go together in making up our belief systems. The irrational, emotive side of beliefs is what gives them the autonomous, self-validating property mentioned in Chapter 1. Beliefs are so resistant to change, because they are composed of thought-feeling feedback loops which influence the manner in which we store and process our sensory experience. That is, our belief systems tend to bias our experiences in a manner which supports the validity of our belief systems. Worse yet, we tend to define ourselves in terms of our beliefs: I'm a Catholic; I'm a Democrat; I'm a moral person because I don't drink (and therefore, by implication, those who drink are somehow not quite as moral as I . . .).

We'll consider the effects of belief systems and other cognitive problems in greater detail in Chapter 8. For the time being, imagine moving toward your goal and locate any values, viewpoints, biases, subjectivities, issues of faith, and other patterns that might stop you from reaching it. Here are some examples we've run across.

Richard would truly like to be hypnotized. He needs to have his wisdom teeth pulled, but he's highly sensitive to pain, allergic to Novocain, and hates the out-of-control feeling he gets from nitrous oxide. But he doesn't believe he would be a good hypnotic subject and despite the fact that his dentist is proficient in hypnosis, that belief seriously inhibits him from entering a trance state.

Above all things, Mr. Johnson would like to have a good relationship with his daughter. He believes that extramarital sex is degrading for a woman involved in such a relationship, embarrassing for her entire family, and sinful in the eyes of God. However, his daughter has just told him that she has been, and plans to continue, sleeping with her boyfriend.

Todd simply wants to be happy. But somehow he has a habit of looking at the negative side of things. He is the sort of fellow who believes that every silver lining has a cloud. And he is *not* very happy.

STEP 8: Are there external forces which might keep you from reaching your goal? What people might stop you? What circumstances might stop you?

Technically, external forces are not a part of the barriers model. The goals you set should be realistic with regard to your life circumstances and the people with whom you've chosen to deal. If you think your goal may be unrealistic, return to Chapter 2 and choose a more reasonable one. Barrier analysis is powerful, but it isn't magic. Neither author of this book, for instance, will *ever* run a 3-hour marathon.

However, locating problem people and problem circumstances can certainly help you access internal barrier elements that might previously have been elusive. So, as an additional aid in your barrier analysis process, imagine moving toward your goal, and then list people and circumstances that you think might hold you back.

Pick the person or circumstance you think might be most responsible for keeping you from reaching your goal. Now, beginning with Step 3, locate the internal barrier elements catalyzed by that particular individual or circumstance. What might you see that would stop you? What might that person say (or what might you hear in the situation) that would stop you? What might you say to yourself about that person/circumstance that might stop you? And so on. Treat each external force you list in a similar fashion.

If you haven't located many barrier components so far, this step should help you. For instance, Ann, a non-practicing Catholic, found herself very much in love with a Jewish fellow named Mike. Dating him had been fine, and when they'd gone to bed together she'd thoroughly enjoyed it. But when Mike popped the question, she panicked!

All Ann came up with during barrier analysis was a

vague but powerful fear relating to getting married. She couldn't link it to Mike in any way, and as far as she could tell she did believe in the institution of marriage and very much wanted to experience it herself.

We asked Ann what external forces might be keeping her back. She couldn't think of any herself, so we suggested some old standbys.

"Your mother?"

"My mother would *love* to see me get married. And she's crazy about Mike."

"Your father?"

"My father's dead," Ann said quickly. But at the same time her body went rigid, and the color in her face deepened a couple of shades.

"If your father were alive, specifically how might he stop you from marrying Mike?"

Ann's eyes and mouth gaped open simultaneously. "God, my father would roll over in his grave if he ever thought I would marry a . . ." Then a whole series of emotions flashed across her face: she managed to look embarrassed, angry, rueful, and surprised simultaneously. "That's terrible!" she said, almost to herself. "Poor Mike!"

Ann went back through barrier analysis with a reincarnated father sitting on her shoulder helping her out. Suffice it to say she had no problem coming up with material the second time around.

We hasten to point out that we do not consider a dead father an "external force." More accurately, he represents a subself, a member of Ann's inner family. But, as was stated earlier, in regard to the barriers model, we wouldn't consider a live father an external force either (unless he actually used physical restraints). Granted, he might have considerable influence to trigger powerful internal barrier elements. But barriers are programmed response patterns that exist inside an individual, and the concept of an "external force" is simply a tool we use to help people recognize the ways they stop themselves from reaching their goals.

STEP 9: **Survey steps 4-8, adding, deleting, clarifying, and detailing as needed. Circle critical elements at each step. Again imagine moving toward your goal. Which barrier element(s) do you run into first? Then what happens? Which elements seem to trigger which? Establish one or more *sequence(s)* of critical barrier elements. Pay particular attention to sequences which form *loops*.**

Sequencing is the summary step in barrier analysis. Your job is to extract what you believe to be the major, or critical barrier elements from the material you collected so far, and arrange them into one or more bioprogram sequences. There is no "right" place to begin or to end, and really there are no "right" answers. Barriers are complex patterns with many interconnections. Approximate sequencing usually works for reprogramming purposes. Whether or not the barrier patterns you come up with accurately represent or even remotely resemble your internal processes is irrelevant. In barrier work (and, we imagine, in most situations) the only thing that matters is the outcome.

In practice, barrier programs often loop back on themselves to form vicious circles. Be particularly careful to locate such patterns. Alternatively, some sequences intersect with other bioprograms that have nothing to do with the goal you've set. And some, of course, just lead up blind alleys.

If you haven't worked with barrier analysis until now, we strongly suggest that you do this step, at least, with pencil and paper. Play around with patterns and sequences, always checking them out against your own experience, until you find one or two that seem to "fit" with what actually goes on inside you when you think of moving toward your goal. Run the pattern through your mind a few times to make sure it continues to make sense, and to check that you've left out no major elements. (Stored sensory experience is far too complicated for you to be able to record every element in the sequence. There would be dozens or hundreds at least; don't even try. Stick with the ones that seem important to you.)

One of our clients described a rather complicated circular sequence to us recently. When we told her we'd probably include it in our book, she thanked us for giving her the left-handed compliment of the week. Here is a summary of what she told us.

Toby wants to ask her boss for a raise. She considers herself underpaid, but she's been putting it off, and is getting more and more annoyed with herself for not standing up for what she believes is rightfully hers. So she sits at her desk rehearsing, saying to herself, "Don't be afraid! Square your shoulders, go in there and ask!" At the word "ask," her anxiety goes up, and she sees an image of a small girl asking a man for money. Suddenly a woman rushes into the scene, slaps the child across the face, and begins to scold in a loud, critical voice. The child hangs her head. Toby feels her back go tense and gets a rush of adrenaline. She has a very fleeting image of her boss looking angry and turning away. She feels a combination of fear and hurt. She sees herself getting her purse and gloves, and leaving early for lunch. A brief feeling of relief washes over her, which immediately triggers a critical voice in her head saying, "You can't chicken out again, you stupid little coward!" She hangs her head for a moment, feeling beaten. Then she takes a deep breath and firmly says, "No, I just have to ask him this time. Don't be afraid! Go in there and just ask him!" Her anxiety goes up. She imagines rising and moving toward his office door, and visualizes a small girl asking a man for money. Suddenly . . . (etc).

We did mean to compliment Toby. Her ability to describe the sequence so well indicates that she has done some serious and successful barrier processing. Moreover, the vicious circle she detailed contains a wealth of reprogramming material. Toby might now begin to work on one or another of her negative self-statements, including the useless commands she repeats over and over. Telling oneself, "Don't be afraid," for example, is about as effective as telling oneself, "Don't think of blue." Or she might focus her attention on sources of anxiety-relief, such as the image of herself leaving early for lunch.

When we worked with Toby we concentrated first on her use of the word "ask," which accessed childhood memories or fantasies of helplessness and criticism linked with physical abuse. Specifically, we suggested that Toby reframe (change her viewpoint about) the goal she'd set. Rather than *ask* for a raise (Boss, can I please have a raise, can I, huh?), she was to get her boss to help her solve a problem (Boss, I have a problem I'd like you to help me with. I'm beginning to feel like I'm underpaid for the work I do here.)* Reframing her goal in a way that didn't bring up threatening memories was *one* of the strategies that finally helped Toby apply for and receive a raise in pay.

The Net Analogy

Throughout this book we speak of sequences of barrier elements, and compare these sequences with the structure of computer programs. We find the analogy to be useful, but we certainly don't mean to suggest that the human mind works its magic in simple linear sequences. A set of experience elements such as the ones listed above occur so rapidly as to be nearly simultaneous. Some of the behaviors can be sequenced, and some of the sensory elements can be *roughly* sequenced; but they don't form single linear strings. Further, the sequences that do exist loop back on themselves and/or connect with one another so often that, visually, the result might look more like a net than a rope.

As a matter of fact, we use the "net" analogy when first describing barrier systems at our workshops. We ask participants to imagine that they are separated from their goals by huge, incredibly complicated 3-dimensional (or n-dimensional) interlacings of habit and experience. "Trying" to reach a goal, then, would be like struggling toward it through the net. The harder you struggle, the more entangled you become. Barrier analysis might in-

---

*This is another example of the "I have a problem" technique presented in Chapter 2.

volve becoming aware of the individual ropes and interlacing patterns; and then picking certain critical lacings to work with. Reprogramming involves the delicate and judicious use of, say, nail scissors to sever the lacings, one by one.* You snip this one, you snip that one—and for a while it seems like nothing is happening. But the structural integrity of the whole net is weakening. Then you clip one more critical lace, and a huge hole appears. Clip a couple more, and the entire thing collapses from its own weight, leaving you free to walk over it to your goal.

Often our problems are so complex that we become entangled in them even as we struggle for solutions. The value of this "net" analogy is to remind us that we can approach them step-by-step, making discrete, repeated cuts here and there, until the whole thing dissolves. In addition, the net lacings form repeatable patterns; once we learn to recognize these patterns we have a shorthand way to formulate what we're up against when it comes time to reprogram. So keep the net analogy in mind—if nothing else, it may help you remember not to struggle toward your goals when there are better alternatives available.

Sometimes barrier analysis itself functions as a reprogramming strategy. As in goal specification, the new awareness may spontaneously produce behavior change. For instance, once Toby is aware that her reticence to ask for a raise is in part a response to the dictates of her own beliefs, her natural stubbornness or her resentment of the

---

*This is the way computer programmers go about debugging programs that aren't running properly. First they download the program onto paper or a video screen, and then study the list of program statements to see what might be wrong. Next they rewrite the few statements they think may be causing the problem, reload the whole program, run it, and see what happens. They do this over and over, if necessary, until the program runs properly. The process is largely one of trial-and-error.

boss could motivate her to say to herself, "The hell with this—I'm a woman now and can do what I damn well please!" and ask for her raise despite feeling anxious about doing it. In other cases awareness alone is insufficient to produce change. However, once the barrier patterns have been uncovered and made consciously available, reprogramming is often a simple and straightforward process.

We now offer a detailed, annotated example of the barrier analysis process. As in Chapter 2, the case is presented in interview format. This is pretty much the way we teach barrier analysis in our workshops, where we demonstrate with a couple of volunteers in front of the group before asking the rest of the participants to use the worksheets on their own.

The following example was taped during a clinical interview. It's been modified somewhat to protect the identity of the interviewee, and to help us clarify certain procedural points.

The Case of Peter

Peter was an aggressive, intelligent young California real estate broker whose specific complaint involved an unwillingness to return phone calls. Each evening he would dutifully make a list of the telephone contacts he needed to initiate the following morning, and another list of the incoming messages which had collected on his telephone answering machine during the day. But when he awoke, he would inevitably procrastinate, paying bills, writing letters, reading the morning paper, or just sleeping in, until it was time to meet a client in the field. Peter was able to make and return enough calls to keep his business going, but felt that his barriers to using the telephone were severely limiting his financial and professional potential.

SPECIFIC GOAL:

WHO: Sales prospects, especially men. John Saunders, apartment house owner.

WHAT: Make a business call, soliciting a listing on his apartment house.

WHERE: My office.

WHEN: 9 a.m. Monday morning.

HOW: Body relaxed, voice sounding confident, assertive.

GENERAL BARRIERS:

Procrastination
Uneasiness about telephone
Self-criticism

Q1: We'll begin now. Remember to tell me whenever you get any reaction at all—a memory, a feeling, anything. If I say "telephone" and you see a glass of beer float by, tell me, OK? Close your eyes. It's 9 a.m. and you enter your office. If you had no problem calling Saunders, what would happen now?

Q1: Goals and general barriers having already been discussed, interviewer begins at Step 3. A fantasy technique is used to stage-set. Questions of the form, "If . . . (your barriers were gone) . . . how would you act?" are often useful at this point.

A1: I'd sit down and call him. He's a hot prospect. I know he's thinking of selling.

Q2: OK. You're dialing the phone, Saunders is answering, you can hear his voice . . .

Q2: Implied is, " . . . pay attention and tell me (or record) what you experience."

A2: I just flashed on my paper lying in the driveway. Thought of the Sporting Green (the sports section), thought of and almost tasted coffee. That's what I'd do—I'd go get the paper.

A2: Peter gives a sequence of sensory images and the avoidance behavior they might lead to. All these are barrier elements.

Q3: OK, good awareness. One avoidance pattern ˙ you might use at this point would be to put down the phone and get the paper.

A3: I do that a lot.

Q4: Now keep your eyes closed, in front of the phone. Focus on this awareness: "I can think of the paper and coffee, and still get ready to call Saunders." (30-second pause.)

Q4: The interviewer is saying, "Be aware of these experiences, and continue to move toward your goal. What else might happen that could stop you?"

A4: That makes me nervous.

A4: A feeling element, but stated in general terms. At this point, interviewer might choose to specify what Peter means by "nervous." For instance, she might ask, "Specifically how do you know you're nervous?"

Q5: Good. Don't try to figure that out, just be aware of it. (10-second pause.) You're going to call Saunders. Picture that. Reaching for the phone, picking it up . . . what's happening?

Q5: In this case she lets the generality stand and goes instead for additional information.

A5: I'm dialing; it rings . . . Saunders answers . . .

Q6: How do you know that?

Q6: She does decide to specify the general statement, "Saunders answers," using a form of the "How do you know . . . [what you just told me] . . . ?" question. The question is intended to help the interviewee restate his answer in sensory (see/hear/feel) terms.

A6: Well, I hear a man's voice saying . . . no, first there's the click of the connection being made, a slight static . . . that sound, it's sudden; makes me more nervous. (Chuckles.) I think I was hoping no one would answer.

A6: Supplies deleted material that otherwise might have been lost. Barrier analysis sometimes involves going back over and over a particular experience in order to get a complete picture of the program sequences and patterns involved. In this case the interviewer found two pieces of information that may be important: (1) that the phone "click" helps trigger Peter's nervousness; and (2) that, probably to reduce his anxiety, Peter imagines ("hopes" means visualizes and/or says to himself) that Saunders won't answer.

Q7: So you dial, it starts to ring, you feel a little nervous, you say to yourself, "Maybe no one's there." You . . .

Q7: Interviewer tests her assumptions and requests additional information.

A7: Something like that . . . I also count the rings. It's a sort of game: the more rings, the better my chances that no one will answer. That's really stupid . . .

A7: Avoidance mechanism; belief element; self-criticism. Interviewer has several choices here.

Q8: That's perfect! We're finding out exactly what you do to maintain your fear of telephones. Do you feel or say, "That's stupid" while you're calling and counting rings?

Q8: Redefines Peter's discovery of a "stupid" pattern as a victory (a most valuable tactic!). Begins to specify the very general self-reference, "stupid."

A8: I don't think so . . . I'm feeling apprehensive, and it sort of helps to get my mind off the call. It just felt stupid when I told you about it . . . for a grown man to . . .

A8: Peter probably feels stupid while on the phone as well. Note that reference to "a grown man" in this context implies that Peter has a child part as well as a critical adult part interested in his telephone behavior. Again, interviewer has many different ways to go at this point.

Q9: OK, good. Thanks for not using that feeling as a reason for holding back. Now you're calling . . . the phone's ringing, you're feeling apprehensive, counting rings, saying, "Maybe he won't answer." What are you visualizing?

Q9: Barrier analysis is an uncomfortable process—reward yourself (or the person you're assisting) at every opportunity for being willing to go through it.

Interviewer asks for visual images, since Peter hadn't been supplying any. He might not be visualizing much—or he may be ignoring the most threatening (and therefore probably the most important) source of sensory experiences.

A9: Nothing that . . . no, I'm seeing his face.

A9: Another deleted element.

It took the interviewer about ten minutes to complete an initial survey of the various pathways that were leading Peter away from the telephone. Then she went back to zero in on what she thought were critical areas. ("Critical areas" are program sequences that seem as though they might be important. There's no real way of knowing for sure: trust your intuition and, as always, take what you get. If you work with a particular barrier pattern and nothing happens, or you find yourself going to sleep in the middle of barrier analysis, then you're probably on the wrong track. Unless, of course, you use fatigue as a way of avoiding uncomfortable situations.)

The interviewer has now completed the initial run-through, and is going back for more details.

Q10: You're sitting in front of

Q10: Returning to specify

the phone about to call Saunders. You imagine dialing, the phone ringing, ringing . . . there's a click, the sound of a connection being made, he says "Hello?" How are you feeling?

"nervous" and/or locate other feeling elements.

A10: Uh . . . a little nervous.

Q11: How do you know you feel nervous?

Q11: The, "How do you know. . . ?" question again.

A11: Well, my breathing speeds up, butterflies in my stomach, tension in the shoulders . . .

Q12: Good; what else?

A12: I'm leaning forward, hunched over the desk, generally tense. When he answers I sort of take a breath and hold it. Think of hanging up. Feel the pressure to start to talk, think, "He might be annoyed that I called."

A12: A rich sequence of sensations and behaviors. Interviewer could pick from half-a-dozen leads here. In particular, note that Peter holds his breath and that he anticipates annoyance from Saunders. Both could be focal points for reprogramming later on (as could several other elements Peter mentioned).

Q13: Specifically how would you know if he were annoyed?

A13: Oh, his voice might sound cold, rushed, hurried . . . I'd get an image of him looking

A13: Peter describes a worst-possible fantasy, and then his rational part takes over. This

impassive and turning away. Looking disgusted. Worst possible, he might say something like, "I wish you damn salespeople would stop calling me." But I know he wouldn't say that.

Q14: How do you know he wouldn't say that?

A14: Well, I know that he's been thinking of selling his building . . .

Q15: So rationally you believe that he might even welcome your call, or at least not resent it too much.

A15: Sure.

Q16: But someplace inside you there's an irrational part who is really afraid that the worst possible might happen, and who responds to that possibility by getting tense and holding his breath . . .

is now Peter tries to reassure himself. We don't have to tell you how little good it does him.

Q14: Interviewer respects the rational part. Then she asks him to specify "know."

A14: Peter continues rationally with a thought. Thoughts are usually conclusions derived from processing complex patterns of sensory data, images, and self-statements. Interviewer could choose to explore this material (e.g.: "How do you know he's thinking of selling. . . ?") and break it down further, or . . .

Q15, 16: She could begin to help Peter separate his rational and irrational parts. Usually these fellows/gals occur in pairs.

A16: I guess there is. Like the scared little kid who doesn't want to get yelled at or put down. Even though objectively I have absolutely nothing to lose by calling the guy and getting it over with one way or the other.

A16: The child part Peter referred to indirectly in A3.

Q17: Right. Now let's go over it again. Specifically how will you know when the scared little kid begins to stick his head up? What specific feelings, sensations, images and self-statements will show you he's around?

Q17: Interviewer will now spend time specifying barrier elements and patterns that are contributed by Peter's "scared little kid."

Were Peter working alone, he might decide to end barrier analysis for the time being and begin reprogramming one of the problem sequences he's already found. By no means has he explored all the patterns that are keeping him away from the telephone and out of a higher income bracket, but he's certainly found enough material to play with if he wants to. If he's unsuccessful, he can always come back for more.

For instance, Peter could use one or another of the tactics described in Chapter 5 to break up some of the critical sequences that seem to be keeping him stuck. On the behavioral level, he might train himself to respond to the sound of a telephone with regular breathing, relaxation, and positive self-talk (arranged in appropriate sequences). If a good visualizer, he might remember or construct clear mental pictures of smiling, pleasant faces answering the telephone. After practicing until he could

call them up at will, he would then work to associate these
images with the sound of a telephone connection, or possibly with his own "nervous" feelings.

However, the emergence of a child part suggests that
there may be an important component within Peter's barrier system. That is, further analysis may isolate an association between Peter's here-and-now concerns and a
negative experience from his recent or distant past. (Obviously there always is such an association at some level.
But the fact that Peter came up with a "scared little kid"
more or less on his own suggests that in his case the
association may be fairly accessible and, if handled effectively, may help to make reprogramming quicker and
easier.) For demonstration purposes, the interviewer now
helps Peter explore further in this area.

Q18: You've called Saunders
and he is upset. Fantasize that
. . . (15 second pause) . . . his
voice is cold, hard . . . you can
see his disgusted look; he's
turning away . . . What does
he look like?

Q18: Interviewer is careful to
use words and images (for the
most part) that Peter has already supplied. Barrier programs are composed of specific words and image content—
change them at all and the
power and accuracy of the
process suffers.

A18: I've never seen him.

Q19: That's OK; just describe
the image in your mind and
then elaborate on it a bit.
You've introduced yourself,
told him whom you represent.
He interrupts you coldly, in
THAT tone of voice . . .

A19: Gray hair, 50 to 55, very distinguished-looking, impeccably groomed, very well-dressed, gray business suit . . .

Q20: Whom does he remind you of?

Q20: This is a good tactic for exploring memories. First specify the image in sensory terms, then ask a question in the form of, "Who (what) does he (she, this place, etc.) remind me of?"

A20: Not my father! (Laughs.) He was short and bald. (Pause.) You know, I have this image of the Successful Businessman—had it ever since I was a kid. That's him.

A20: Remembered images don't have to be "real."

Note the emergence of humor at this point. The humor, of course, could mean anything, but often signals that a connection has been made. Of course, an intensification of negative feelings may also suggest that something meaningful is happening.

Q21: Successful Businessman—that's great. Hyperconfident, does mysterious things with lots of money, Raider tickets on the fifty-yard line, moves three steps above it all.

Q21: Interviewer elaborates on the "Successful Businessman" stereotype using some of her own associations (in apparent contradiction to the suggestion at Q18). However as she does so she watches Peter carefully; if her suggestions don't seem to match his image she'll be quick to take them back.

A21: Right.

Q22: Just the kind of guy who would have no time for or patience with a scared little kid playing real estate broker . . .

A22: Really!

Q23: Think back now. Does that image remind you of anyone in particular? Anyone you know? A character in a movie?

A23: Not really . . . no, wait. This may be a little far-fetched. There was a guy I used to caddy for when I was about ten or eleven. I never saw him in a suit, but he used to act that way. He used to ask advice and then turn away before I had a chance to answer.

A23: The most far-fetched associations are sometimes the most valuable ones. Some of our clients locate useful "past life" memories (images that apparently originated during a previous lifetime) during barrier analysis. Believing in past lives often has little to do with whether or not such "memories" can work for you. They may be fantasies or metaphors that have a great deal of relevance to *this* lifetime, no matter what their origin. So if they come up, suspend skepticism and use them.

Q24: Specifically, how did you feel when he treated you that way?

Again, Peter may continue to explore memory associations, and integrate what he finds into their appropriate
places within his emerging barrier structure. He may then
continue with barrier analysis, or instead select a reprogramming strategy to deal with past images that seem to be
fouling up business calls. For instance, in using active
fantasy or hypnosis he might "return" to the past in his
current (adult) form and help his eleven-year-old self deal
more effectively with his reactions to the Successful Busi-
nessman-Golfer. We call this the Big Brother/Sister technique, and have used it effectively in dealing with a wide
variety of irrational fears.

Procedural Guidelines

Leaving Peter to his telephone, we now present a set
of guidelines that may help you apply barrier analysis
more easily on your own. As was stated earlier, there is a
lot of room in this process for intuition, innovation, and
variations in individual style. We purposely presented
Peter's work in interview rather than in worksheet format
to underscore the point that the steps in barrier analysis
need not be done in any specific order—on the contrary, if
you try to "cookbook" the process you may lose a lot of its
value.

1. *Write your work down.* After you're more familiar with
   the process you'll find yourself doing it automatically,
   "on the hoof," to deal with problems as they arise.
   But while you're learning it, record what you do. This
   will be particularly valuable when you wish to recycle
   back through the various steps.

2. Barrier analysis is a *repetitive process.* Be willing to go

through the necessary steps many times, tedious
though that may be.

3. *Scan the entire pathway(s)* between your present state
   and your goal, looking for major barrier elements
   before getting detailed information about one particular element or pattern.

4. *When in doubt, specify* memories, beliefs, and other
   patterns into their component sensory elements, and
   then sequence the elements. Sometimes larger structures can be handled effectively as units. But we've
   found that, when barrier analysis or reprogramming
   doesn't work, it is most often because something has
   been left unspecified.

5. *Accept approximate sequences.* It is rarely necessary
   (and next to impossible) to get an exact and stable
   sequence of elements. The same work done tomorrow
   would most likely yield a different sequence. Also, it
   usually isn't necessary to sequence an entire barrier
   program (such as Peter's). Work with critical chunks
   and patterns.

6. *Don't begin reprogramming too quickly.* This is a most
   common error. Among other things, it limits the
   potential changes to be gained from barrier analysis
   alone. Let it happen, give it a chance.

7. *Trust your intuition.* If you get the feeling that a particular element or pattern is critical, then it probably is.
   Often, patterns that are the most uncomfortable to
   specify turn out to be the most critical during reprogramming.

8. *Respect your parts.* Barrier analysis may get you in
   touch with some parts of yourself of which you
   weren't previously aware, and may not like very

much. Respect the right of all your parts to be heard, and make room for all opinions and viewpoints expressed. If necessary, go back to Chapter 3 and do additional inner family work before moving on.

9. *Reward yourself frequently* for your willingness to go through the barrier analysis process. At best it is a tedious job, and at worst it can be downright painful. So mix a good many pats on the back in with your processing and note-taking. You deserve them.

SUMMARY

Barrier systems are bioprograms that stop you from reaching goals you set for yourself. Essentially, barrier analysis helps you compile precise and useful answers to the question, "What stops me?" Barrier analysis will help you uncover specific sequences of behavior and sensory experiences that lead you away from what you believe you want. These sensory/behavioral sequences can be dissolved and reprogrammed much more easily than can the more general, subjective issues that people usually focus on when trying to improve themselves.

In some ways barrier analysis is a tedious and exhausting process. But it's also one that you will get better at as you practice. After a time, the analysis procedures you use when you work on yourself will begin to "streamline": that is, you'll no longer have to think about every step, but will begin to do portions of the process automatically. In addition, you'll gradually become familiar with common patterns and sequences that get in your way. You'll learn to recognize critical elements much more quickly and will begin to move automatically from analysis to reprogramming.

A final word: in our work we rarely do as complete a barrier analysis as the one described in our last example. Usually we train our students to barrier-analyze only until they've found a couple of critical sequences they think might be worth programming. Many students quickly begin to do analysis and reprogramming more or less simultaneously, moving back and forth from one procedure to the other as necessary. While you're learning the techniques of barrier analysis, we suggest that you proceed formally, as described in this chapter. But, as with any other skill, you'll quickly find yourself personalizing them into a set of tactics that best fit your own individual needs.

4

Parts Analysis

In the past forty or fifty years a truly frightening number of books have been written about the causes and cures of inner conflict. It is certainly not our intention to replicate those efforts here. Yet conflicts do seem to keep a lot of people from getting what they think they want out of life. Neither the most precise goal specification nor the most exhaustive barrier analysis will help you much if part of you is afraid or unwilling to make the changes they call for. Knowing *what* to change doesn't do much good if you haven't decided *whether* to change.

In our experience, goal ambivalence (a conflict between inner family members regarding the specified goal) leads either to procrastination or, worse, to forced change. We trust most of you are familiar with the effects of procrastination. Not only is the work not getting done, but now the self-loathing you feel for being the way you are is accompanied by feelings of guilt for not getting off the dime. Forcing change can have several serious drawbacks. First, we just don't think it works very well. Forced changes take more time and effort to make than "agreed-upon" ones. Second, they tend to wear off. The exercise kicks and fad diets last for three weeks; then the weight begins to come back on. Third, forced change can lead to increased intra-psychic conflict. That is, the parts of you that don't want the change begin to resent the parts that are forcing the change to occur. This in turn can cause increased stress, symptom substitution ("The diet's going fine, so why am I tired all the time? And what about these hives?"), and/or a variety of other related problems.

Our message is this: don't procrastinate and don't try to force yourself to change. Deal with your ambivalence instead. To that end, we now present a process intended to help you reduce, or at least partially outflank, goal-related conflicts. In this chapter we leave the workings of the biocomputer for a time and focus instead on the "self," the operator of the biocomputer. On you. To do so, let us return to the Inner Family Model mentioned briefly in Chapter 3.

Parts Analysis is a fantasy process designed to help you decide whether or not you really want to reach the goals you defined on Worksheet 1. Specifically, you will contact the part or parts of your inner family that is/are responsible for maintaining your barrier patterns and keeping you from reaching your goals. You will then ask these parts to help generate agreements or solutions that will serve their needs and let you as a team work toward reaching your goals. If you are able to come up with a strategy or compromise that satisfies "all of you," and if your parts agree to proceed, then you're on your way. Before proceeding, we should mention that it is not necessary to believe that you really have a lot of little parts running around inside you. The Inner Family Model simply provides a metaphor, a way of organizing your experience of yourself. However, acting as if the subselves really exist seems to facilitate the process of identifying and dissolving barrier systems. So we suggest that, during inner family processes, you treat your parts as if they were real people and give them the same deference and respect you would give a real family.

PROCEDURES

Parts Analysis was designed to be done in fantasy. We suggest that you read through the descriptions and examples provided in this chapter and then learn the steps well enough to do them from memory. However, if you are someone who doesn't work well in fantasy, simply use pencil and paper. How you do this process doesn't matter as long as you do it in a way that works well for you.

STEP 1: **Review the work you've done so far. Imagine trying to reach the goal you specified in Chapter 2. What stops you? List the most important barrier patterns isolated in Chapter 3.**

Joanne's goal is to give up smoking. Specifically, she would like to relax with her family over morning coffee with her hands empty in her lap or wrapped around breakfast utensils (as opposed to a Virginia Slim). She imagines doing so and feels anxious. She continues to imagine not smoking at the breakfast table, visualizes her husband lighting up a cigarette, and becomes angry. The tension in her body increases, and she can almost feel herself reaching for a cigarette.

Jerry imagines telling Todd that she'd like to date other men. She sees him slam out the door, and then she begins to tell herself what a fool she's been for throwing away such a comfortable relationship. She feels frightened and wants to stop the exercise.

Randy's goal is to start his own consulting firm. He imagines leaving his current job and feels a vague, depressing ache. Randy doesn't understand why: he *hates* his current position. He continues to imagine starting his own company, and the dull ache simply continues. It doesn't seem related to anything.

STEP 2:   **Close your eyes and focus inward. Find the part of you that is responsible for the barriers that are keeping you from your goal. Allow your sense of that part to deepen and expand until you have a clear image of him/her. Give the part a name if appropriate.**

It is most important at this stage to relax, let go, pay careful attention, and take what you get. People inexperienced with doing this kind of fantasy work often have preconceived notions about what a subself responsible for a particular barrier system should look like. Very often the part in question will manifest itself to you in a most unexpected manner. You may experience a visual image, a sound or voice, a sensation, a feeling, or any combination of these. Simply go inside, try to imagine that a part of you really is responsible for keeping you from your goal—and then see, hear, or feel what happens.

If you get nothing at all, it is permissible to create the image of a subself. Sometimes this is very helpful the first few times you do inner family work if you need to get the process off the ground or to troubleshoot when it stops for some reason. However, the absence of a part image may be significant in itself, and you should reserve the active creation of a particular subself to use as a last resort. Learning to use the inner family model is a little like learning to play a musical instrument: the richness and depth of the experience usually increases with practice (though some people seem to get plenty of richness and depth the first time around).

The following images have all been described to us as representing inner family members: a colorful, swirling bowl of gas;* a baby in a womb seen from a great distance; a feeling of apprehension accompanied by a slight tensing of the stomach muscles; and a low roar entwined in a dull red sash. Of course, a great many parts appear as people, of all shapes, sizes, and ages, and of either sex. (Some of your parts may not be of your sex.) Nor are these image manifestations necessarily stable. Sometimes parts will change dramatically in the manner in which they appear to you during parts analysis.

As mentioned above, you may name your parts if it seems appropriate. A much better alternative, of course, is to ask a part what its name is—you may already know—and then use that. If the part has no name, or if it won't tell you its name, then giving it one is optional. Some people simply use descriptions (my angry part, my baby part, the

*All your parts are "people," but sometimes they may communicate with you in visual images or other non-verbal patterns.

part of me that wants to remain single, etc.). When you're working with several subselves and are recording your work, or if you are working with someone else, names sometimes help a bit to keep things straight.

One caution: avoid derogatory nicknames. Treat your parts with deference and respect—consider them valued teammates. It is singularly difficult to maintain respect for a part of yourself that you continually refer to as "Dummy." Yet the inner families of many people contain self-critical parts who tend to label other inner family members in just that way. For instance, Mary, the woman afraid of parties (Chapter 1) named one of her more conservative parts "Yellow Streak." Her intent was partly ironic, and it didn't seem to hinder her progress any (we think). But we let her get away with it primarily because we didn't know any better at the time. Though there are exceptions to every rule, it is usually best not to call your nastiest parts anything you wouldn't want to be called yourself. (After all, keep in mind who they are!)

STEP 3:   Ask the part, "What is your purpose in keeping me from attaining this goal? What are you trying to get from me or save me from? How are you trying to serve me by holding me back?" In other words, uncover the part's positive intentions in keeping you from your goal.

We believe that all behavior is positively motivated and that all continuing behavior has a positive payoff. We also believe—and this is of critical importance—that your parts are not out to get you. They are on your side. Their purpose is to serve you. Although they keep you from breaking up with Janet, paralyze you with fear at the slightest thought of public speaking, or send you to the kitchen for a second piece of cake, these are negative side effects of their strategies. Their intentions are to serve.

We all tend to criticize ourselves for our "faults." We put ourselves down for being fat, for not saying hello to the attractive stranger at the party, and so on. We make those parts of ourselves wrong and cut them out of our consciousness. We alienate them and treat them as enemies. And by doing this we also lose the many positive resources that these inner family members may have to offer. We throw the baby out with the bath-water and must face the world with impoverished resources and a lessened sense of self. We literally become "unactualized" or "unwhole."

Consider Phil, who came to our workshop to learn how to get along better with women. Thirty-five years old, he had never been married, and he was aware enough to know that he had serious barriers toward members of the opposite sex. In addition, he presented himself as a most somber and proper fellow. He wore a sport coat and tie to the workshop, knowing that most participants would be dressed casually. And during our sixteen hours with him we didn't see him laugh more than twice. His questions and small-group interactions were to the point, but academic and intellectualized.

During the inner family process, Phil located a part of himself that seemed responsible for keeping him away from women. The part was very parental—and when he asked it, "How are you trying to serve me?" it responded, "Don't you remember? Can you imagine how horrible it would be if you took a woman home with you and then wet the bed that night?"

It seems that Phil had been enuretic until about the age of ten. During high school and college he'd been deathly afraid of being found out, and among other things he developed a mild secondary impotence. He remembered both the enuresis and the impotence but hadn't previously connected the two. But much more dramatic for him was the fact that he hadn't connected his early enuresis with his inability to get along with women and his generally somber nature. A child part of him wet the bed? Then he would bury that part! He would lock it away forever under a set of inhibitions that left him stiff, formal, and above all things, adult and dry. His child part understood and played along but didn't like it one bit. And, of course, the richness and joy that the child in each of us brings to our lives was not available to Phil.

Again, as in Phil's case, barriers were erected to serve a certain function. Here are some other positive intentions that can motivate apparently negative and self-destructive behavior patterns. A part of Sally keeps her fat to provide a ready excuse for being rejected. Were Sally thin and *then* rejected, she would have no recourse but to accept herself as the truly rotten person her mother always told her she was. Errol locks his knees during the heat of a racquetball game because he's learned he'll probably do OK by playing that way. A part of him is afraid that if he tried a new way, he'd miss the shot, blow the game, and really prove himself a loser. Jerry doesn't break up with his girlfriend because a part of him believes, "If I let her get away, I'll never find another one. Besides, I would hurt her feelings, and only bad people hurt other people's feelings." He wishes neither to be a bad person nor to spend the rest of his life alone.

STEP 4:   Ask the part, "Will you help me look for ways to serve your intentions while also allowing me to reach my goal?" Continue to focus inward and pay careful attention to any response.

In trying to perform effectively, most people tend to commit what may be called the "Either-Or Fallacy." (See Chapter 8.) This fallacy is a mental set that provides only two ways of viewing and responding to a particular situation. The parts of us responsible for maintaining our barrier systems are usually mired neck-deep in some variation of the "Either-Or Fallacy."

For instance, John is writing his first novel. An irrational part of him believes that his book will either be a success or a failure. Fearing the latter, that irrational part forces John to procrastinate, keeping him from experiencing the shame of having written a lousy book. Although John's rational mind may be aware of other alternatives— writing a fair-to-middling book, writing a poor book and not being ashamed, etc.—the irrational part of him is not. So John is left with putting things off and wasting time for reasons that he doesn't even understand.

John could probably figure out all of this if he were to use the inner family model. At this particular point, he would ask his part, "Part, would you be willing to help me look for some ways that I could finish my novel and also keep myself reasonably safe from devastating embarrassment?" Now, John's part may not believe that any such alternative exists. As a matter of fact, there may be no such alternative. But John can ask—and if his recalcitrant part is willing to bring its resources to bear on the problem, or if John is freer to use some of his other creative resources, then another option may be found. For example, he might hire a copy reader to check his final draft and okay the manuscript before it's sent out to the publisher. Sometimes no easy solution is available, but it never hurts to look around for one.

Let's return for a moment to Phil. In the course of his inner family work, Phil found that there were really two parts involved in maintaining his barrier system: the enuretic child he located in Step 3, and an authoritarian figure that was responsible for holding the child in check in order to prevent embarrassment. Phil asked the latter whether it would be willing to look for ways to give the child-part more freedom without risking the horrors of a soggy morning after. He then asked the child-part whether it would be willing to look for ways to be more active without risking the embarrassment of enuresis. The child-part said, "I'll help look, but I don't think there are any. And if I screw up, that sumbitch up there is going to stomp me sure!" The child-part's ambivalence notwithstanding, Phil now had two concerned but valuable resources on his team as he began to search for ways to loosen up around women.

We should make it clear at this point that your parts are not necessarily agreeable to change. They usually say that they'll help look for alternatives that might break up the Either-Or dilemma and that, if acceptable, they might be willing to help implement such alternatives. We suggest that you reassure them that you will not go ahead and attempt change strategies without their permission. And we most emphatically suggest that you then keep your word. Fantasy, auto-hypnosis, and other intrapsychic strategies are very powerful tools. We believe that they should *never* be used to manipulate a subself into changing a position or a point of view.*

STEP 5: If the answer is "no" or otherwise ambiguous, ask, "Are there any conditions under which you might be willing to help look for alternatives?" If the answer is "yes," specify the conditions.

Ideally, your parts will be at least tentatively willing to cooperate with you if you go about contacting them in the manner described above, carefully reassuring them that your intent is non-manipulative. Even when you get an initial "no" there may be conditions under which the reluctant part would be willing to cooperate with you.

For example, Carol committed herself to writing a chapter for a book but found that she kept procrastinating and was not getting the writing done. During the inner family process she discovered that the part of her preventing her from working on the chapter—Carol named the part "Jane"—was afraid she'd get so involved in the writing process that she would begin to neglect her marriage. Carol asked Jane to specify conditions under which she would be willing to let Carol write the chapter. Jane said she'd be willing to help only if Carol would figure out a way to guarantee her husband equal time no matter how involved she became in her work. Jane feared that once

---

*There are those who would disagree with us on this. For example, hypnotists have paired aversive hypnotic suggestions with bad habits, e.g., "The next time you try to smoke a cigarette you will become violently ill" and have successfully reduced the incidence of the habit. However, such tactics are absolutely contrary to the philosophy and applications presented in this book.

Carol started writing, she would become so enslaved to the project that she would have little or no time for her own personal life. Carol said that she would be willing to set aside three evenings a week to spend with her husband and do no writing at all. In addition, she promised to talk the situation over with him, tell him about her fears regarding writing and time commitment, and get an agreement from him before she proceeded. Once these conditions were specified, Jane was willing to make an unqualified positive commitment to help Jane find ways to finish her chapter.

Sometimes it's appropriate to define conditions even when the part in question has already agreed to help you look. For example, Phil was concerned about the pessimistic feeling expressed by his child-part during Step 4. When he asked the child if a conditional agreement might help, he got an immediate, energetic, and very unexpected response. "Sure," the child replied. "I'll come out and play with you if you agree not to sleep with any women for awhile." Somewhat taken aback, Phil nonetheless agreed and a contract was quickly struck. Phil told the entire workshop that he had agreed not to have sexual intercourse for a period of six months, and in return his child-part had agreed to help him learn to be more open and spontaneous with women in other ways. Actually, Phil was only agreeing to have another six months like his last six months (sexually)—but this time it would be by his own choice, a profound difference indeed. No longer would he criticize himself horribly every Friday night for not hitting the singles bars and acting "like a man." No longer would he feel that, if a woman seemed even remotely receptive, he had to push the issue and follow through if possible. Free from those pressures, he would be much more likely to try out new behaviors that his child-part might suggest.

Actually, we think that Phil and his child-part came up with an elegant therapeutic strategy, one that a trained professional would have been hard-pressed to surpass. This example is just one of many that we've seen of the quality of self-healing that can occur when an individual is able to stop fighting within him/herself and get back on his/her own team.

STEP 6: **If the answer is still 'no," redefine your goal to reflect the decision not to change for the time being. Your new goal may involve learning to accept that decision while you work in other areas of your life, or it may evolve spontaneously from the inner family work itself.**

For inner family work to be anything more than a hollow ritual, your parts need the freedom to choose to cooperate with one another in their own time and in their own ways. And it is important that you respect your parts in whatever decisions they make. They're on your team, even though it may not always seem that way. It is important to choose to accept a decision of "no change" and to take responsibility for it. This process is an active, positive one ("I choose to weigh 150 pounds right now and to like myself that way!") rather than a defeated, negative position ("What's the use? I can't stick to a diet—I'm such a weak, undisciplined person!"), that ultimately leads to further inner conflict and low self-esteem.

Accepting a decision of "no change" may seem like something of a hollow victory. But consider these issues:

First, choosing not to change is a temporary decision, made in the interest of self-respect and in the anticipation that additional work will be done. Second, it may be more of a victory than you think: the process of active yielding sometimes turns out to be a pathway to a most dramatic and observable positive change. When it happens between two people, we call the process "assertive yielding." That may seem like a contradiction in terms. It's not.* In Chapter 2 we mentioned the Aikido master who, in attempting to throw his opponent, finds himself being thrown. At the moment that he senses that the fortunes of leverage and balance are turning against him, he chooses to be thrown. He concentrates on being thrown perfectly, blends harmoniously with the energies involved, and completes the movement in a position that leaves him best able to make his next move.

Sometimes old goals dissolve and new ones emerge during the inner family process. Usually that means that the goal you began with wasn't really yours at all, but rather was sold to you by someone else. Minor habit changes (fingernail biting) and skill acquisitions (learning to play bridge) often fall into this category. ("*I* don't want to learn to stop biting my fingernails! My *wife* wants me to stop biting my fingernails. I *like* biting my fingernails!") Sometimes, though, the issue is not so minor. A man that we know had been asked by his wife to consider open

---

*Some of these concepts don't make a lot of sense when viewed from a western perspective, but they've been deeply embedded in eastern philosophy for thousands of years. An ancient Zen parable on the value of yielding, updated for barrier analysis, might run something like this: "To the extent that I *need* to change I find myself powerless, imprisoned by the shackles of that very need. But when I am willing to let go of changing, give up my need to be different, and accept myself simply as I am—in that very act of yielding I find myself free to do and be whatever I choose."

marriage. She wished to be polygamous and strongly urged him to sleep around as well. The concept made him acutely uncomfortable, but he agreed. Then he sought counseling, hoping to learn to conquer his "prudishness and sexual insecurity." During the inner family process he realized that it was his wife's preferences, not his own, that were making him uneasy. He located a part of himself that was afraid that if he verbalized his strong desire for mono-gamy his marriage would be in danger. In order to save the marriage, that part had agreed with his wife that he should learn to enjoy multiple relationships. He'd been criticizing himself for weeks over his inability to do so. When he realized that he simply wanted to be monogamous, he felt as if a great weight had been lifted from him. Of course, he still had to deal with his wife's polygamy (which didn't particularly threaten him *per se*) and the strain that her polygamy and his continued monogamy might put on their relationship (which did threaten him). Still, his new awareness left him much less self-critical and in a better position to attack some of the problems, choices and emo-tional upheavals that obviously would await him further down the road.

STEP 7:   **Focusing inward, ask, "Are there any other parts of me that might stop me from finding a way to reach my goal?" If the answer is "yes," return to Step 2 and proceed.**

As you work, remember that the abstraction we are calling your "self" can be divided into as many parts as you have viewpoints, tastes, biases, subjectives, priorities, preferences, and goals. An inner family process this week might be completely different from one conducted next

week, even though precisely the same problem is involved—and yet both sessions might be equally successful. Human consciousness can be ordered and processed
in an infinite number of ways. Above all, don't assume
that there is only one part of you interested in the outcome
of a particular goal specification/barrier analysis. Different parts may emerge from your "self" at any point; they
should be acknowledged as friends and team members and
then be dealt with appropriately at the time. Often it will
be necessary to recycle repeatedly between process steps
or to otherwise modify the specific outline given here.

Generally speaking, keep the following two points in
mind and you'll do well. First, run your inner family
processes in ways that are meaningful to you. Remember
that your ultimate aim is to explore and reduce inner
conflicts that may undermine the barrier analysis and
reprogramming strategies through which you hope to better your life. Parts Analysis is a pragmatic process designed to have a specific effect and to help you achieve a
specific outcome; use it that way. Second, remember that
whatever comes up is right. You may not like what you
find (e.g., a part of you that you consider hateful) or
understand what you find (e.g., a lot of confusion and
mixed messages) or even believe what you find (e.g., a part
of you left over from a "past life"). Nevertheless, the most
important single rule for successfully utilizing any intra-
psychic process is: "Pay careful attention and take what
you get."

**STEP 8:   Warmly acknowledge all your parts for their
            help and support. Though sometimes their
            viewpoints and survival tactics may have**

negative consequences, their intentions are
to serve you.

Always end an inner family process session on this
positive note. Remember that the inner family is a metaphor after all; what we are really talking about is *you*
thanking *you* for being *you*.

Mary and the Ski-Singles

The following example comes from a worksheet
completed by Mary, the lonely woman who is afraid to
attend parties (Chapter 1). In this case, Mary's goal involves attending a ski-singles meeting where she's heard
there might be some attractive men. As before, we've
annotated Mary's work and edited it somewhat for clarity.

STEP 1:   **Imagine trying to reach your goal. What
might stop you?**

GOAL:

I want to go to the Ski-Singles
Club meeting Friday night.

GENERAL BARRIERS

1. I'm too shy and can't
meet people.

2. No one will talk to me.

3. People will feel sorry for
me because I'm alone.

Mary's reasons for wanting
to avoid the meeting are fairly
complex. On one hand, she's
afraid she'll be ignored and
suffer an agonizingly lonely
evening in the midst of a
roomful of people enjoying
themselves. On the other
hand, she's terrified that
people *will* notice her and pity
her or inundate her with unwanted   attention.   This

4. I'm scared I'll meet a creep.

5. I'm scared I won't meet anyone.

dilemma is a good example of how the Either-Or fallacy can create a no-win situation. Given that Mary believes she'll lose either way, it's no wonder she wants to avoid the meeting.

STEP 2:   Focus inward. Locate the part of you responsible for erecting and maintaining the barriers that are keeping you from your goal. If appropriate, give the part a name. (Avoid strongly negative labels if possible.)

I notice a knot in my stomach and I get a fleeting image of a small child behaving like a coward . . . I'll call her Yellow Streak.

We asked Mary to expand her impression of Yellow Streak and see if she could come up with a name that was less judgmental. Labels are surprisingly powerful: if Mary gives this part of her a weak and cowardly name, she is that much more likely to feel powerless. She is also more inclined to feel disapproving of this part of herself instead of seeing the part as being on her side.

When I look again, I see the scared little girl and she reminds me of myself when I was about five years old. My dad used to call me Marcy—his nickname for me—so that's what I'll call her.

STEP 3: Ask the part, "What is your purpose in keeping me from my goal?"

1. If I stay home, I won't have to face being rejected by an attractive man.

2. I won't have to deal with saying "no" to someone I don't want to spend time with. (I know I wouldn't be able to do it.)

3. I won't have to face other people's criticism or pity. Even if they wouldn't say anything, I'd be able to tell what they're thinking.

4. If I don't go, no one will be able to think I'm loose or on the make.

5. If I go to the meeting, then I'll have to go to my friends' parties or they'll feel hurt.

6. If I go, I might meet a great guy and start a relationship, only to have him leave me just when it will hurt the most.

As Mary questions Marcy, she discovers quite a few reasons why Marcy wants her to stay away from the Ski Club. Notice that these reasons do not have to be particularly realistic. To Marcy, the scared little girl inside Mary, they are very real indeed, and she is determined to keep Mary safe from rejection and hurt.

STEP 4: Ask the part, "Will you help me look for ways to serve your intentions that also allow me to reach my goal?"

Marcy is worried that she's going to be ignored if we go off looking for other answers—after all, the rest of Mary might get reckless and throw caution to the wind if Marcy agrees to help out. Mary forgets how scary it is out there. So, I don't know . . .

Notice the Either-Or fallacy: either Marcy has to be in charge and keep Mary from going out, or the reckless side of Mary—actually another "part" we contact later—will take over and cause a disaster. The response to the question is ambiguous, a common response at this point.

STEP 5: If the answer is "no" or otherwise ambiguous, ask, "Are there any conditions under which you might be willing to help look for alternatives?"

Yes! Marcy says that as long as she still has the right to object to going to the meeting after all the alternatives are explored, she'd be willing to help look. I'm willing to give Marcy right of refusal, if she's willing to help look for new alternatives.

Good for Mary! Remember, the commitment at this stage is only to help explore other options, not actually to go to the meeting. Marcy needs to be reassured that Mary will not force her to do things that are unacceptable to her.

STEP 6: If the answer is still "no," redefine your goal to reflect the decision not to change at this time.

I'll go ahead and meet Marcy's conditions.

Mary does not have to change her goal, since she did reach an agreement within her inner family. If she had met with an adamant refusal,

Mary's job, at least for now, would have been to accept the decision of "no change" and to feel good about herself for making that choice.

STEP 7:   Ask, **"Are there any other parts of me who might stop me from finding a way to reach my goal?" If the answer is "yes," return to Step 2 and proceed.**

I just got a very strong reaction to that question: there's a part of me called Private Person who's afraid I'm going to forget how important time alone is to me. Once I start going to meetings and parties, he's afraid I'll lose my ability to recoup and recharge myself. . . . Okay. Private Person is willing to help look—if I can guarantee that I'll never cheat him out of the private time he knows I need.

"Private Person" is a subself quite distinct from Marcy and has different intentions and motivations in dealing with Mary. Now that she is aware of him (Mary seems to have a male identity for Private Person), she can recycle through Steps 2-7 with him in mind.

STEP 8:   **Warmly acknowledge all your parts for their help.**

I had no idea that there was any good in this tendency of mine to shy away from social events. I guess I've spent a lot of time hating myself for

No comment necessary. Do it!

"chickening out" of opportunities to meet men. It's kind
of hard to shift gears now and
actually feel grateful to that
side of me . . . but I'll give it a
try. Thanks, Marcy.

SUMMARY

Sometimes goal specification and barrier analysis are
enough to help initiate a desired behavioral change. When
they're not, some ambivalence or conflict is usually involved. Although generally uncomfortable, this inner
conflict may not be readily apparent to the conscious
"self."

When people experiencing inner conflict force themselves to change, the process is usually difficult, the effects
may wear off, or the process may not work at all. In
addition, side effects (anger, resentment, somatic com-
plaints, and so forth) may, in the long run, make things
worse than they were to begin with.

Parts Analysis provides a practical, straightforward
method in helping you become clearer about what you
really want to do. It is a fantasy process that uses the Inner
Family Model to help you explore parts of you that are
resisting change.

Parts Analysis is based on three assumptions:

1. Your various viewpoints, biases, and goal conflicts
   can be ordered into parts or subselves that in some
   ways resemble an actual family.
2. The parts of you that are responsible for maintaining
   your barrier system and keeping you from your goal

are not your enemies. They are on your side and are operating, as far as they know, for your benefit. Their intentions are to serve you. However, the negative side-effects of their service strategies happen to be keeping you from reaching the goals you've set for yourself.

3. You are willing to work cooperatively with your parts to bring about the change. Parts Analysis is not to be used, indeed, was never intended to be used, as a device to help you manipulate or hypnotize yourself into changing.

Parts Analysis will help you utilize the resources of your entire self, thus enabling you to seek methods for overcoming barriers and to reach specified goals in a manner that serves you best. Up to now we have presented our model of inner family work in a fairly sequential format. As you become familiar with the purpose behind this process, you'll find yourself dropping some of the steps, possibly adding some of your own, and in general streamlining the entire package to fit your individual style and needs.

SECTION II
Reprogramming Strategies

5

Sequence Reprogramming

In Chapter 3 you learned how to analyze your barrier systems into discrete patterns. In this chapter you will learn how to modify these elemental sequences so that eventually they will lead you toward rather than away from your goal. Essentially, this involves adding positive elements at critical points in the barrier pattern.

For example, Joan says to Heidi, "How would you like to introduce the next conference speaker?" Heidi blanches and then erects (largely outside of her own awareness) a very rapid barrier sequence.

She sees the audience in front of her, feels her stomach tighten, feels herself go blank, says to herself, "Oh-oh, I won't be able to remember his name," feels herself begin to panic, sees the audience begin to get restless, feels/hears herself stutter and begin to fake the introduction, and feels flushed, embarrassed, and trapped. Simultaneously, she remembers what she'd been planning to do at that time: help Nancy at the registration table. She sees herself there, laughing, relaxed, counting ticket stubs, feeling the relaxed pace and lack of pressure. She compares the two feelings, and tells Joan, "I'd like to, but I think Nancy still needs me outside."

Again, Heidi is unaware of most of this as it occurs. Were she asked to recall her experience at that moment, she might say, "Well, I felt a little nervous about introducing a speaker, and I remembered that I was supposed to help with registration." And she truly wouldn't be aware of much else.

Barrier analysis allows Heidi to become more fully conscious of this barrier sequence. At that point she is ready to reprogram.

In a barrier sequence each element serves to activate, or "trigger" the element which follows it, just as the sight of food may be said to trigger salivation in a hungry dog. In Heidi's case, the self statement, "I can't remember his name" triggers a feeling of panic. The sight of the audience in front of her triggers stomach tension. And so forth.

To reprogram the sequence, we must hook a positive response (a feeling or action that will help Heidi perform successfully) to one or more of the sequence elements. Hopefully, this will cause an association which will lead Heidi toward rather than away from her goal.

For example, in this case Heidi might be given an index card containing the speaker's name and professional affiliations. Now, the card by itself may not help much. People who in the throes of panic can barely remember their own names can easily forget that they're holding cue cards. So our next step is to "install" the use of the cue card into Heidi's barrier system.

We might have her stand on an empty stage holding the index card. She would then say to herself, over and over again, "I can't remember his name" and then look down at the card in her hand. After many such pairings, the statement itself will remind Heidi to look down. We might then have her imagine the room to be filled with an audience, and have her repeat the same process several times. Finally, we might have her make the same association fifty or a hundred times in a room full of real people.

Alternatively, we could have Heidi change her self-statement from, "Oh-oh, I can't remember his name," to "I can't remember his name *on the card in my hand.*" This retraining procedure is very easy to do, though, of course, it must be practiced many times.

At any rate, once the process is complete the internal sequence Heidi runs through when she is asked to introduce a speaker will be different. Now when Joan makes her request, Heidi will see the audience in her mind's eye, feel her stomach tighten, feel herself go blank, say to herself, "Oh-oh, I can't remember his name *on the index card in my hand,*" look down at the index card, see his name, and murmur, "Thank God, I've got it here . . ."

Although this one change probably will not be sufficient to overcome Heidi's reticence to introducing speakers, it will help. Now a second reprogramming procedure can be tried, and a third. Eventually, Heidi will have little trouble when she anticipates getting up on a stage.

Please keep in mind that this and the other examples presented in this chapter have been taken out of context. For instance, we do *not* mean to imply that Heidi's public speaking anxiety can be dissolved completely and permanently with simplistic reprogramming strategy. Human behavior is complex and highly resistant to change. No doubt Heidi possesses dozens of barrier sequences that contribute to her affinity for the registration table. And some of these contain emotional reactions which, at best, will only change over time.

To summarize, one of Heidi's public-speaking barriers (the verbal and feeling components of "going blank") will now activate a new behavior (looking at the cue card) that will help decrease rather than increase her aversion to public speaking.

While we're on the subject of anticipations, let us underscore one additional point before moving on. Our primary intent is not to help Heidi become more comfortable when introducing speakers. Our intent is to help Heidi feel more comfortable and confident *when Joan asks her, "How would you like to introduce the next speaker?"* Heidi's particular barrier system includes the prediction that she will forget the speaker's name. After successfully completing the steps we described above, Heidi will feel less nervous when she anticipates introducing a speaker. She knows that now, at least, she'll give the proper name and affiliations. With that confidence, she will be more willing to take a chance.

For those of you who consider that something of a hollow victory, consider the millions of people who could do reasonably well on a stage, on the phone, on tests, or when meeting prospective in-laws—but never try, or try and fail, because they become so badly shaken at the anticipation of the event. That's one of the things that makes assertiveness training classes so popular. Countless people sit in restaurants quietly eating burnt cow because when they think of complaining they become so anxious they never call the waiter. They all know how to send improperly cooked steak back, and waiters almost always comply with such requests. Yet there are thousands of pounds of overcooked meat eaten every year in this country simply because anticipatory barrier systems are so effective in keeping goal-directed behavior from occurring at all.

Now let's take a look at the specific steps involved in sequence reprogramming.

PROCEDURES

Sequence reprogramming is easy to do but sometimes takes a while to complete. The hard part is conducting an accurate and exhaustive barrier analysis. Once critical sequences have been uncovered, the next step is often so obvious that you will begin to reprogram automatically. In other cases it takes some conscious effort. For the remainder of this chapter we will assume that you are already competent at goal specification and barrier analysis. If you're not, maybe you'd better go back and practice more before moving on.

We suggest that you follow these steps the first few times you try sequence reprogramming. However, as you become familiar with the procedures, no doubt you will adopt a more streamlined progression that works well for you. As before, these steps are taken from worksheets that we use in our training seminars.

STEP 1:   Review the goal you specified in Chapters 2 and 3.

You should be absolutely clear about where you're

going before you try to get there. Be sure that your goal is stated in who/what/where/when/how form.

STEP 2:   Referring to your barrier analysis, pick a critical sequence of barrier elements with which to work.

Carefully review the structure of the barrier or habit pattern that's holding you back. Pick out a specific sequence or pattern that seems to play a central role in keeping you from reaching your goal. This is the pattern you'll begin to reprogram.

STEP 3:   From this barrier sequence pick a specific trigger-response pair to reprogram.

As we've said before, barrier programs work like chain reactions. Each element in the sequence is activated by the element preceding it and in turn activates the one immediately following it. Study the sequence you described in Step 2, and pick a pair of elements that seem to play a particularly important role in holding you back. From now on, the first of these will be called the *trigger element*, and the second, the *response element*.

In the example given earlier, Heidi's negative self-statement, "Oh-oh, I'm not going to remember his name," possibly acting in tandem with the feeling of "going blank" (sometimes feelings and self-statements occur simultaneously) was the trigger-element we chose. The response element was Heidi's feeling of "beginning to panic."

STEP 4:   Choose a substitute response element—one you believe will be more effective in helping you reach your goal.

Assuming for the moment that you will not be able to avoid the trigger itself, how would you like to respond to it? Specifically what would you like to see, say, feel, or do instead of what you now see, say, feel or do? In what way could you respond that would help you instead of hurt you? This is the pattern you will now try to pair up with the trigger element.

At this point you might ask, "Why not just erase the trigger element? That's what seems to be causing my problem." That is an option: you can begin reprogramming anywhere along the barrier sequence. However, in practice, some barrier elements turn out to be much easier to change than others. For instance, criticism produced stomach tension, which in turn triggered off defensive behavior in a female trainee. It would have been nice if we could have taught her to relax her stomach while being criticized by, say, her husband. That is certainly what all the books suggest. Unfortunately, she'd been trying to learn how to relax her stomach for years, but still couldn't do it when she felt antagonized. Possibly biofeedback or some other strategy could help her in that regard, we don't know. But in our workshop this trainee found it far easier to use stomach tension as a trigger for responding with empathic listening and other non-defensive behaviors, rather than try to get rid of the tension itself. Now when her stomach tenses she automatically listens and then (if appropriate) says what she feels—rather than defending herself. (And her stomach is gradually becoming less tense when she feels criticized.)

There are numerous ways to reprogram. Again we repeat, the bottom line is choosing something that works well for you.

STEP 5: Practice the new response until you can do it automatically, without having to think.

In the face of stress, people tend to revert to old habit patterns. In such cases, in order to install the new response pattern in your barrier program, you are going to need to know it cold. Practice it under low stress conditions until it becomes second nature to you.

You'll find this step much more important in some cases than in others. Successful reprogramming of this type actually depends upon two things:

1) whether you *know how* to employ the new response pattern when your barrier program is running, and

2) whether you *remember* to employ the new response pattern when your barrier program is running.

For example, Heidi knows how to look down at an index card no matter how frightened she is—she doesn't really have to "learn" her new response. On the other hand, someone who is learning to negotiate needs to practice and learn the various diplomatic tactics involved before he will be able to use them effectively under pressure in an unrehearsed situation.

STEP 6: Pair the new response elements or patterns with the old trigger.

We suggest that you do this in fantasy at first, and then, if appropriate, in "real life" situations. The program installation is complete only when the trigger element automatically produces the new response element instead of the old barrier element. Depending upon the situation, this can happen fairly rapidly. But remember, many habits are deeply ingrained and resistant to change. Sometimes the practice phases of sequence reprogramming can take weeks or even months.

There are a great many pairing strategies available for your use. Which ones you'll choose will depend on the specific problem under consideration, and on your own preferences. These strategies are generally based on common sense and we leave the specific development of pairing techniques to you. However, here are some common variations. Let's say that this time the goal involves maintaining eye contact in the face of criticism.

1) Both the trigger and the new response can be experienced in fantasy. I clearly visualize my boss dressing me down while I watch him in a calm, confident manner.

2) The trigger is imagined and the new response is actually practiced. For example, I look in the mirror imagining that my reflection is my boss. Imagining clearly that he is criticizing me, I maintain eye contact with my image and say out loud an assertive statement I've chosen to practice, such as, "I believe that criticism is unwarranted."

3) You can practice a new response in fantasy while experiencing a real trigger. Your roommate dumps three weeks of stored-up frustration on you. Though not ready to confront her quite yet, you listen carefully while clearly imagining that you're maintaining eye contact and speaking assertively.

4) Both the trigger and the new response can be real. For example, practice maintaining eye contact with coffee shop waitresses while ordering food.

5) The trigger and/or the response can be imagined or acted out in exaggerated form.

6) A variation we'll be talking about later involves duplicating the trigger element and then changing it in some way. For instance, imagine the boss dressing you down. As you make and maintain eye contact, you suddenly realize he is naked and sitting on a toilet seat.

As stated earlier, pairing strategies are legion. Be willing to experiment in order to find the ones that work best for you in your particular situation.

STEP 7:   Test the program installation. Try to reach your goal, and pay careful attention to what happens.

If you are able to reach the goal you set earlier without much trouble, congratulations! You are better at this than we thought. If you manage to reach your goal, but still experience some discomfort from the old barrier system, return to Steps 4-6 for more practice.

If you didn't reach your goal, pay careful attention to what stopped you from doing so. Then return to Step 2 and proceed. Or return to Step 1 and further specify your goal. Or in some cases it may be best to try a different programming strategy altogether—one that more closely fits your priorities and personal style.

Once one trigger-response linkage has been disrupted and a new, more adaptive response installed, pick another important sequence and work on that one. At first, nothing may seem to be happening to the overall barrier system; however, as more and more of its component sequences are altered it will weaken. Eventually it will collapse—just as a fish net collapses of its own weight when enough of its interlacings are cut—and reaching your goal will be easy.

Spontaneous Recovery

So, you've worked hard, and you haven't let this lengthy process get you down. You've finally learned to make those skiing turns with elegance and grace. But then that night you have a few glasses of wine, sleep like a log, hit the slopes the next morning in time for the first run— and suddenly your turns are worse than they ever were! What the hell is going on here?

One of the most frustrating things about reprogramming is the occurrence of what psychologists call "spontaneous recovery." Basically old habit patterns are like poor relations: they tend to return without being invited just when you think you've gotten rid of them for good. So remember this. Spontaneous recovery is a natural part of the relearning process. It does not mean that you've failed as a reprogrammer and as a person, and must go back to taking what life dishes out to you. Just keep working on the same old patterns. After a while you'll notice that each successive time a barrier system "spontaneously recovers" it is weaker. Eventually the unwanted pattern will disappear completely, and you will be rid of it once and for all.

Let's now turn to a specific example of sequential reprogramming.

Brian: Dealing with Anger and Criticism

Brian is a soft spoken, rather inhibited, "boyish" man in his late twenties who took our workshop in order to learn to deal with other people's anger. As it turned out, the "other people" were translated to specifically represent men, around whom Brian felt inferior. With women he could be both charming and assertive, and was not particularly sensitive to their criticism. But when he had to deal with men who were older or physically larger than he, or whom he classified as authority figures, his behavior changed markedly. He became timid, seemed unsure of himself, and literally blanched at the first sign of aggressive or critical behavior. When unable to avoid such confrontations, he would simply shut up and passively agree with whatever was said to him—while deep inside hating himself for his response. At best, he would make feeble attempts to turn the other men's anger into a joke at his own expense.

It probably won't surprise you to learn that Brian's father criticized and yelled at him a lot. The father lived in Florida, 3,000 miles away, but Brian still cringed with the fear of incurring his wrath or, ultimately, being rejected altogether.

The following material is taken from Brian's reprogramming worksheet. We've modified and summarized it somewhat to make the example easier to follow. As you read on, please remember: there are many ways to do barrier analysis and reprogramming. The work Brian did with us is not necessarily the "right" way; it just happens to be the way his case proceeded at a particular workshop on a particular day. If our training seminar had been a week later, the direction he chose to follow may have been quite different.

Having presented that disclaimer, we hope that these excerpts from Brian's worksheet may serve as guidelines for you as you begin to reprogram your own barrier systems.

STEP 1:   Restate your general and specified goal.

GENERAL:

I want to be less intimidated by aggressive men.

SPECIFIC:

WHO: Ralph G., an associate at work.

WHAT: I want to be able to tell him how I feel when he yells at me. "I don't like it when you use that tone of voice. I don't want you to yell at me."

WHERE: Anywhere at the office.

WHEN: The next time I see him. Then, immediately after the next time it happens.

HOW: Strong, firm voice; relaxed body; good eye contact; without defending or arguing.

About a week prior to the workshop, Brian asked Ralph, a department head at the office (about two job levels above Brian, but not in the same chain-of-command), if he would like to sit in on the demonstration of a word processing machine Brian wanted the company to lease. To Brian's amazement, Ralph immediately began yelling that Brian had no right to authorize such a demonstration (untrue) and that he was trying to horn in on his (Ralph's) end of the business (also untrue). He ranted and raved at Brian for a good five minutes in front of several office workers, and then stomped out of the room. Brian, on his part, could do nothing but quietly agree; and a couple of hours afterwards he called Ralph to try and smooth things over. Inside, of course, he was angry and hurt. He believed he'd been wronged, but felt helpless to do anything about it.

STEP 2: Describe the barrier sequence you would like to work on, and list, in sequence, the major elements involved.

GENERAL:

Ralph began yelling at me and I froze up. I didn't know what to say or do. It reminded me of times my father used to yell at me. So I played patsy again.

SPECIFIC:

1. I see Ralph's face becoming flushed and angry.

2. I hear him yelling.

3. I remember my father.

4. I feel myself wilting, getting smaller.

5. I feel like he's leaning over me.

6. I see my father's face superimposed on Ralph's.

7. I feel frightened, contrite, helpless.

8. I agree with Ralph, but I'm speaking to my father's enraged face.

Brian's worksheet contained more than twenty programmed elements, many of which we left out. Notice that the sequencing isn't precise: For instance some of these items may have happened simultaneously. But it's approximate, and that's good enough for reprogramming purposes. Also, notice how Brian used a general memory (item 3) to access a specific here-and-now visual image (item 6) and feeling state (item 5). Obviously, these are cornerstone elements in Brian's barrier system. Again we mention that the sequence Brian "downloaded" here is simplistic and grossly incomplete when compared to the internal experience it is intended to represent. Also, it's probably wrong. Regardless, notice how rich it is in useful lies. Even with this small amount of data, Brian could start to reprogram in three or four different areas.

9. I hear myself sound like
an intimidated little boy.

STEP 3: Pick a specific trigger-response pair to re-program.

TRIGGER:

I see my father's face super-imposed on Ralph's.

RESPONSE:

I verbalize agreement, feeling like an intimidated little kid.

Brian chooses to reprogram his reaction to Ralph's/his father's face. He's not going to work on the fact that he's con-fusing an intimidating mem-ory with the here-and-now experience (although he cer-tainly could do that).

STEP 4: Choose and describe a substitute response element.

I want to tell Ralph/Father how I feel when he yells at me and to stop doing it. I'll say, "Ralph, I don't like it when you yell at me in front of other people. Please don't do that."

Brian's choice to meta-communicate here is of course a valid one. However, if feel-ing-talk happens to be inap-propriate at his particular place of business, Ralph can choose a variety of other re-sponses. In summary, we would ask him to choose three or four different programming variations and have him prac-tice all of them. One substi-tute response might include emotional behavior: pounding a pillow and screaming to the image of his father's angry face, "Get off my back!"

STEP 5: Describe how you will practice a new response.

1. I'll role-play it with some people in the shop.

2. I'll practice it in front of my wife, you'll be able to tell me how I sound.

We suggest that you practice even this simplistic a pattern for quite a while before moving to Step 6. It's amazing how quickly one can go blank in the face of a powerful emotional trigger. In order to overcome that old learning, you must have the new response down absolutely cold. In other words, your biocomputer must be able to produce it automatically on cue, with virtually no conscious help from you. More complicated response patterns, such as active listening or a tennis back-hand, require hours and hours of practice.

STEP 6: Pair the new response element with the old trigger. Describe how you plan to practice.

1. I'll imagine my father's face and voice until I actually begin to feel intimidated. Then I'll make my statement out loud if there is no one else around.

2. I'll get someone here to yell at me; we can role-play the situation again. I'll conjure up

Brian plans to use both fantasy and "real" triggers as he practices; this is usually the most powerful approach to use. Incidentally, remember that Brian is reprogramming himself to deal with Ralph's, not his father's, aggressive behavior. As a matter of fact, Brian doesn't have any parti-

my father's face and overlay it on the guy who's practicing with me.

3. I could call my father and ask him to help me. I'm probably not up to that, though . . .

cular bones to pick with his 1980 father. It's his 1955 father, all spittle and whiskers and meanness, leaning over him and screaming down at him that's bothersome. Of course, Brian associates the 1955 father with the 1980 one, just as he categorizes authority figures with angry men in general. For that matter, Brian could have asked Ralph to help him out. It is often dramatically effective to approach your antagonist and say, "I get intimidated when you yell at me. I know that's silly, but I do. Would you please yell at me some more so I can work on getting over my sensitivity?" This is an advanced technique which double-binds your antagonist while giving you valuable practice. However, like most advanced strategies it can be tricky. We suggest that you use it with care.

STEP 7:   Test your work. Record what happened.

(Brian, of course, was not able to try for a specific goal at the workshop, so he left this and the remaining steps blank. We do know from followups that he's much more able to stand

The proof of the pudding is in the eating after all. No matter how eloquent it may sound, barrier analysis isn't worth its weight in mouse droppings unless it really does

up to people like Ralph than he used to be. We also know that he called his father and told him he planned to purchase a house in California. Brian anticipated that his father would be enraged at his "wasting money at those California prices." Although it made him nervous, Brian told us he was able to call without much hesitation.)

help people reach their goals. So, after reprogramming you test your work. Occasionally the new program sequence runs adequately the first time, and no further practice is needed. Usually, however, several test-practice cycles are required before the new sequence is truly operational. Behavioral change is, after all, a gradual process no matter how you cut it.

As we mentioned in the commentary, Brian could have chosen any number of other trigger-response sequences to work on (though we certainly believe he chose a most important one). For example, he could have paired the sound of Ralph's yelling with the image of Ralph sitting on a commode, straining to complete his business there in the wake of a three-day siege of constipation. Using a verbal tactic, he might have taught himself to paraphrase rather than agree with loud criticism. Or, as we mentioned, he might have answered his father's image with pillow pounding and screams of his own.

Usually more than one trigger sequence must be reprogrammed before a barrier system begins to melt away. Even then it's almost always a case of successive approximations. Complicated, long-standing habit patterns rarely disappear completely. Nevertheless, reprogramming can be valuable. Furthermore, these strategies seem applicable to a wide variety of situations outside the traditional realm of psychology. For example, variations

of reprogramming are being used more and more as training techniques in the world of sports.*

SUMMARY

To review briefly, sequential reprogramming is used
to disrupt the cause-effect chains that occur in barrier
systems. Positive response elements are hooked into the
barrier sequence at critical points in the hope that (1) the
structural integrity of the barrier sequence will begin to
break down, and (2) the positive elements will generate
new program sequences which will be more effective in
helping you attain your goals.

As we define it, reprogramming displays the following characteristics. First, general behavior patterns are
broken down into minute experiential components, which
are then pulled out of context and worked on individually
or in short sequences. This is in contrast to many psychotherapy techniques, which tend to work on more global
levels. In a way, reprogramming strategies may be likened
to piano scale exercises. Though highly artificial and
seemingly mechanical, they do help you learn to play the
piano in a way that simply playing songs never could.
Second, reprogramming emphasizes the dissolving of barriers, rather than "trying" to reach your goals. The assumption is that, once your barriers are out of the way,
you will naturally move toward the goals you'd like to
attain. And third, barrier analysis and reprogramming
give most people a different way to look at the circumstances in their lives. Sometimes these viewpoint shifts are

*For information on sport-related applications, see Galway, T., *Inner Tennis*.

so profound that reprogramming is virtually unnecessary; the desired change occurs spontaneously as the barrier analysis or goal setting is taking place.

In this chapter, we focused our attention on procedures for installing positive elements within barrier sequences. Often this installation will cause incompatible negative elements to melt away. However, in some cases the negative barrier element or sequence is so powerful or so deeply seated that positive responses are difficult to install. For instance, this is often true when strong negative feelings are present.

In the next chapter we will address this difficulty and consider reprogramming strategies aimed at erasing negative elements from barrier systems.

6

Reprogramming
by Duplication

There's an old and oft-quoted story about a man who spent each morning sitting on his roof tearing his newspaper into small pieces and throwing them into the wind. One day his neighbor came over and asked him what he was doing. "I'm keeping the Indians away," came the reply. "Why there are no Indians around here!" exclaimed the neighbor. "See," quoth our hero proudly, "it works!"

Sure, it may be that our paper-throwing friend is a prime candidate for the local cracker factory. But that's only because his irrational fear is more obvious and his survival tactics less sophisticated than those of the people who will put him there. Everyone spends time "keeping the Indians away" in one way or another. And many of us lose a great deal more than newspaper in the process.

As pointed out earlier, barrier programs often fold back on themselves, forming self-rewarding and self-maintaining patterns called "avoidance loops." The fellow in our little story has himself trapped in one such loop. As long as he keeps throwing paper off the roof, he never gets to find out whether or not there are really Indians in the woods. Furthermore, the harder he tries to thwart the uprising, the more deeply enmeshed in the avoidance loop he becomes. And keep in mind: this guy only looks like a nut to people who don't believe there is an Indian problem. Everyone else on the block hires him as a consultant.

The point is that these avoidance loops can be very difficult to break. We saw in Chapter 1 how Mary could choose to spend the evening shivering in her car rather than "risking" entering a party where, in her rational mind, she knew she'd be welcome. To take another example, a fellow at one of our workshops complained that he could never get anywhere on time. And he'd been late coming back to the workshop from lunch. He believed his problem was a lack of time-management skills— he'd taken several training seminars in that area. Unfortunately, his chronic tardiness saw little improvement.

He completed a barrier analysis, and was surprised to discover that he had a chronic low-grade fear of being early. In his fantasy he saw himself coming in ten minutes early for a meeting, then sitting around feeling bored and self-conscious with nothing to do to occupy his time or say to other early arrivers. He was particularly nervous about having to converse with persons in authority. Thus, arriving late for our workshops avoided that worst-possible eventuality of having to spend ten minutes alone in the room with us.

Another of our students wished to become less self-critical. On analysis, she found that her self-criticisms were mainly triggered by the anticipation of being criticized by others. She would then beat them to the punch in order to lighten the blow.

Anticipation of falling is a common barrier in skiing; anticipation of hitting the ball out of bounds causes us to inhibit our tennis swing and hit the ball into the net. Writer's block often derives from anticipation-based fear that the writer will produce a lousy piece of work. Stutterers develop speech blockages by trying so desperately not to stutter, and so on.

When the avoidance patterns in a barrier system are very powerful, simple installation procedures such as those detailed in the last chapter often don't work very well. In these cases, a way must be found to weaken the avoidance loop so that positive options can be installed which will eventually replace the ineffective program. Fortunately we have an effective way to do this: it's called "duplication."

Duplication

Broadly speaking, to use a duplication technique you simply replicate and/or exaggerate the barrier system you are trying to dissolve. You continue to "duplicate" the response pattern until it no longer bothers you, or until you can easily choose not to do it in circumstances where it previously would have occurred automatically. The practicing can be done either in fantasy or in real life, although, when possible, the latter approach generally produces better results.

It may seem paradoxical that reproducing an unwanted pattern will actually help you get rid of it. Indeed, a few years ago a psychiatrist named Allan Fay published a book he called *Making Things Better by Making Them Worse*. In it Dr. Fay discusses the therapeutic effects of paradox, and for illustration gives examples of a variety of duplication tactics that some therapists use in their work. In another book with an apparently paradoxical title, *Giving in to Get Your Way*, by Terry Dobson and Viktor Miller, the authors describe a variety of communication training techniques and self-help procedures based on Eastern concepts which gave birth to such martial arts as Aikido. Dobson and Miller present some very effective assertiveness training strategies; yet at first blush, "giving in to get your way" seems like a strange way to learn to be assertive.

But when you look at it closely, duplication tactics aren't paradoxical at all; or at least they are no more so than most other peculiarities of the human condition. It all goes back to the avoidance loop concept. The stutterer maintains his speech impediment and his fear of performing in public by avoiding public appearances and by trying as hard as he can not to stutter when he does open his mouth. He can resolve his public speaking anxiety, and eventually become more fluent as well, by choosing to speak in public and then stutter on purpose while doing so. After awhile his biocomputer will learn that non-fluency no longer elicits the ridicule it did in second grade, and the occasional negative reactions that do result can be handled with relative ease.

Our friend the Indian fighter uses a variation of duplication called "response-prevention." One morning he climbs to his roof with no newspaper to rip up and throw.

(If he wants to be doubly safe, he asks his neighbor to tie his hands behind his back.) Response prevention helps duplicate negative emotional patterns by eliminating the behavior that is helping you avoid the emotion-producing triggers—e.g., if you throw papers off your roof to keep the Indians away, find a way to prevent yourself from throwing paper off the roof. Our friend then sits quietly and watches the horizon as his anxiety mounts. Eventually one of two things will happen. Either he will die of arrow wounds, or his biocomputer will discover that there are really no Indians out there after all, and that paper-throwing is not necessary for survival.

PROCEDURES

We now present the basic steps involved in duplication. Keep in mind that, as with other reprogramming themes, barrier systems can be duplicated in a variety of ways. Be willing to experiment: as always, it is most important to find the specific strategy variations that work best for you. In doing so, however, we suggest that you stay within the following general guidelines:

1. When possible, duplicate small, specific response patterns rather than large, global ones. As in sequence reprogramming, work on one element at a time. It may feel like nothing is happening for awhile, but as you continue to reprogram individual barrier elements you will be weakening the barrier system as a whole.

2. It's imperative that duplication be carried out within the context of a positive attitude and a lot of reinforcement. Remember, duplication is not usually a

pleasant procedure to use, as it does, after all, require that you repeat behaviors and emotional experiences that you would just as soon forget about. Give yourself plenty of warm fuzzies for having the courage, intention, and self-respect to work in such a powerful and potentially effective way.

3. Once you begin a duplication session, continue it, if possible, until the negative feelings involved begin to lessen. If you start to duplicate, become more upset, and then stop, you run the risk of sensitizing rather than desensitizing yourself to the triggers in question. We'll discuss this problem in more detail later.

In review, duplication is used when sequence reprogramming alone is not powerful enough to help you reach your goals. This is usually the case when a negative behavior or feeling pattern is central to your barrier system. Duplication is then used as the first step in a two-part reprogramming process. First, one or another duplication tactic is employed to weaken the negative barrier system. Once that is done, some other reprogramming strategy can be used more effectively to install program elements that will help lead you toward, rather than away from, your goal.

STEP 1:   **Pick a response pattern that is keeping you from reaching your specified goal, and that you would like to change.**

As you did while goal setting, first describe the barrier system in general terms. The central element may be either a feeling or a behavior, although in every case both feelings and behaviors will somehow be involved. Some common general barrier systems: behavioral habits such as blushing, ticks, stuttering, nervous laughter, aggression; compulsions such as excessive drinking, hand washing, stove checking; fear of such things as flying, contamination, public speaking, failure, height; negative emotions such as anger and jealousy; obsessional thought patterns, and so on.

STEP 2: Specify the following barrier system components: triggers, anticipations, behaviors, and feelings.

It's usually important to do this step in writing. List as many as you can of the elements or characteristics included in each of the four major components of your barrier system.

Triggers. By triggers we mean the specific circumstances, both internal and external, under which the negative pattern you're working on seem to occur. Verbal criticism, the sight of a snake, the memory of a lost loved one, the feeling of hunger, and the condition of being alone all might constitute central trigger elements in a barrier system. As always, specify trigger patterns in sensory terms (see/hear/feel).

Anticipations. Next list any anticipations that may be associated with the trigger elements you've found. Amelia, for example, goes to school anticipating the laughter she knows will accompany her stage performance during assembly. Whenever Todd thinks of calling Martha for a date, he anticipates being turned down. Specifically, he visualizes the disgusted look on Martha's face as, upon hearing his invitation, she rolls her eyes at the ceiling, and sounds vaguely disgusted as she tells him she will be busy in the foreseeable future. George has a fear of heights. He thinks of the drink he's supposed to have with a prospective client on Tuesday evening at the revolving bar 56 stories up in the San Francisco Hyatt. As he does so, he can almost feel the building sway and hear the wind whistling around the tower. He then anticipates his own reaction—breaking out into a cold sweat, beginning to shake—and imagines his client looking on with pity and scorn.

Barrier-related anticipations can be broken down into two categories: "Reasonables" and "Worst-Possibles." In your own work, pay particular attention to the latter and write them down no matter how ridiculous they seem. It is these worst-possible anticipations that are running and perhaps ruining your life.

Behaviors and Feelings. Finally, list the feeling and behavioral components of your barrier system. Record each in sensory terms. It is not enough to simply write, "When I see a snake, I get frightened." How do you know you get frightened? Specifically what do you see/hear/feel that means "fear" to you?

Similarly, it is not enough to write, "I go blank and get tongue-tied when I talk to pretty girls." What specific tension patterns are involved in the experience of being "tongue-tied"? What do you think of (instead of what do you say) when you try to talk to women? Remember the skills you learned while goal setting, and use them here.

A fellow we know (actually we know him quite well— he's one of the authors of this book) had quite a severe stuttering problem. After years of lip service, he finally decided to do something about it—he dove into the therapy literature and began trying out techniques. One which made a lot of sense to him was a variation on duplication called "symptom prescription." So, using symptom prescription, he set out to stutter his way to fluency.

There are, however, two major varieties of stuttering. *Primary stuttering* involves the involuntary repetition of the first sound in a word, s-s-s-such as th-th-th-this. *Secondary stuttering* results when the stutterer realizes he is stuttering, and attempts to control the symptom. It is most commonly manifested in what's called a "block": the victim's face turns red, his facial muscles contort, his body may twitch and jerk, but no sound comes out at all. Anyway, this particular fellow was a secondary stutterer, as are most adults. But when he began to stutter on purpose, he tried to produce a primary-type stutter. Neglecting to specify his *own* speech patterns, he tried to act the way he thought stutterers behaved. Not only was this worthless as far as therapeutic benefit was concerned, but soon the fellow began to block while trying to stutter. That is, he would begin to st-st-st-st- . . . and then his own habit would manifest itself. His voice apparatus would freeze bringing the "voluntary" stammer to a halt. These were black days! Our hero would hang his head dejectedly, and mumble, "God, I can't even *stutter* right!"

The problem, of course, was that he was trying to reproduce someone else's pattern rather than his own. Eventually he sat down with a mirror and a tape recorder and learned to recognize and reproduce his own individual speech and behavioral patterns. He began to duplicate these under a variety of critical trigger conditions, and eventually the technique helped him regain some measure of fluency.

Step 2 is half the battle. It is vital that you learn to duplicate your own involuntary behavioral and feeling patterns, rather than some other patterns which you have misperceived in yourself, have inferred from a general diagnostic label (such as "stuttering"), or that someone else has told you you should be working on. The duplication technique involves doing exactly what its name implies.

STEP 3:   **Specify one or more trigger conditions to begin with. Reproduce them, either in fantasy or in actuality, then begin the duplication process.**

Tactically, duplication is an easy technique to use. All that's required is that you learn to replicate, and then choose to replicate voluntarily, what you're already darn good at doing involuntarily. Duplication can be used for a great many kinds of problems; the specific procedures vary somewhat depending upon characteristics of the issue at hand. We would need a book in itself to cover all these variations exhaustively, so at this point we shall content ourselves with providing a few examples, and describing a few problems and pitfalls that may arise.

Behaviors. When working with a behavior such as a stutter, a tick, a nervous tremor, an aggressive tone of voice, and the like, it is most important to be able to duplicate the actual problem behavior in question. Learning to duplicate an involuntary behavior, however, is not always easy. Most of us are not very aware of how we behave under stress; we must rely on feedback from others. Sometimes problem behaviors are not even recognizable from the inside. So we suggest that you do rely on as much feedback as you can get. Ask a trusted friend to watch you practice until he or she can't tell the duplicate pattern from the original. Use a videotape machine if you have access to one; otherwise a mirror and a tape recorder can be a poor man's substitute. Last, and possibly most important, learn to pay careful attention to your behavior under trigger conditions. The lowered awareness most of us have under stress is itself an avoidance reaction, and undoubtedly is involved in the maintenance of negative habits. Paying attention under stress will not only give you more information about yourself, but will also speed up the change process.

Response prevention is usually the best way to deal with compulsive behaviors, addictions, and the like. The trick is to prevent the compulsive ritual and pay careful attention to what happens instead. Usually whatever does happen will trigger fear or some other negative emotion. However, sometimes a symptom prescription is used instead. A woman who compulsively washes her hands for two hours a day could be required to wash them for *six* hours a day. Alternatively, the symptom prescription can be made contingent on the initiation of the target behavior. That is, the woman is told, "You may wash your hands upon rising, after going to the toilet, prior to each meal, and immediately before bed with no consequence. You are free to wash them at any other time as well; however, if you do, you must continue to wash them for at least one hour." Similarly, a man who compulsively checks the door after he locks it can be required to continue to check it for an hour if he initially checks it more than once. When the compulsive individual is willing to follow such prescriptions, the behavior in question may become so aversive that it eventually drops away. We sometimes use this variation on symptom prescription in conjunction with response prevention, which we still find to be the first and best alternative with most compulsive/ addictive individuals.

Feelings. When working with a feeling pattern, the trigger situation is often a complex intermingling of external and internal experiences. For instance, Mary wishes to be able to say hello to attractive men at parties. External factors which contribute to her anxiety include: the man in question returning her gaze; other people at the party watching her; the fact that the man may be in a group rather than seated alone; and so on. Internal factors include physical tension, body tremors, and other internal sensations; negative self-statements such as, "I look terrible in this dress"; and memories of prior negative experiences with men at parties. Further she is certain she'll make a fool out of herself as soon as she opens her mouth. When Mary actually tries to say hello there will be so many things happening simultaneously that she may become confused and end up blocking out (avoiding) everything.

We would instruct Mary to pay careful attention as she begins her exercise, notice *one* of the things that is making her most anxious, and focus her contentration on that trigger element throughout the interaction. For instance, she might focus on the tremor in her body while she walks across the room to say hello. Should another element suddenly become much more anxiety provoking—for instance the sarcastic comments of a third party—she would switch her attention to the second element, and concentrate on it. Thus, her duplication task might be, "As you say hello and have a brief conversation, focus carefully on the most frightening part of the experience, and let yourself become just as anxious as you can."

This is simply another example of what we've been stressing throughout this book: take a complicated goal, barrier system, or situation and break it down into specific elements; then work on one thing at a time.

Example: Public Speaking

Let us stress at this point that it is very possible to be physically involved in a trigger situation without being experientially involved. As a matter of fact, that's exactly what most of us try to do when we're faced with a frightening task. Unfortunately, it doesn't serve to reduce barrier systems. For instance, blanking out the audience may have helped John squeeze a shakey C out of Speech I in high school without growing an ulcer in the process, but it certainly did not help him significantly reduce his fear of public speaking. A "helpful" teacher had told him that, if he stared at the clock at the back of the room instead of at the class, he would feel less anxious while giving oral reports. So John dutifully stared at the clock while he talked. He didn't die, and he did eke out that C, so his biocomputer drew the conclusion that surviving in public speaking situations meant avoiding the audiences.

But John was dying in his present job, which required weekly team meetings, and where a promotion would be dependent upon a good deal more public speaking as well. So, with commendable courage he threw himself into a self-help program. He took evening speech classes; he practiced in front of his wife and family; he even joined a Toastmasters Club where individuals can be called on to speak extemporaneously, and shuddered his way through three months of meetings. Nothing worked.

When we convinced John that he needed to experience public-speaking exercises rather than simply be physically present at them, things began to change. After a lot of in-office fantasy work, John once again began to venture forth into the public-speaking community. When speaking this time, he intently focused his attention on the audience as a whole, allowing his eyes to move from face to face at random. To keep his anxiety up he did not reassure himself (response prevention). Instead of arguing with or trying to counter negative self-statements, he simply paid attention to them, let them be. If, for one reason or another, an individual in a particular audience frightened him, then he gave his speech to that person. In addition, we used sequence reprogramming, relaxation training, and other procedures to deal with specific aspects of John's problem. Within a year, he was speaking freely and easily both at work and at home. While we don't believe that John will ever particularly like speaking in public, we're confident that the fear of doing so will never again be a barrier to him.

To summarize our last point: when duplicating emotional response patterns, simply going through the motions is not enough. You must clearly and intently experience the various trigger elements in the various anxiety-producing situations with which you decide to deal.

STEP 4:   **(Optional) Exaggerate a critical component of the barrier system in order to intensify the negative feelings or behavioral actions involved.**

Exaggeration is often an effective tactic when reprogramming the anticipation component of barrier systems.

As we mentioned earlier, people frighten themselves with worst-possible anticipations. They then attempt to reduce the resulting anxiety by repressing the worst-possibles, rationalizing them away, or avoiding them in some other fashion. They're often somewhat successful; and the anxiety relief they experience reinforces both the original anticipation and the subsequent avoidance strategy. The result is a person who continues to have worst-possible anticipations, but is only partially conscious of them; and who has also developed a host of reasons/excuses/explanations for his or her ineffective behavior and mediocre life. In these cases the anticipation—irrational and semi-conscious as it may be—contains critical trigger elements which must be dealt with. Insight therapy is sometimes effective in bringing these worst-possibles into consciousness, where they may then be reprogrammed. However, insight therapy is often slow, and can be expensive; as a quick-and-dirty alternative, exaggeration often fills the bill.

Basically, use what you have to help access what you don't have. Allow yourself to become aware of the portion of your fantasy that is conscious. Then systematically exaggerate it, either in fantasy or in real life; allow your anxiety to rise as it will; and pay careful attention to what happens. Do this while experiencing a target situation, in fantasy or (preferably) in real life. As with other reprogramming strategies, be specific, be repetitive, pay attention, and take what you can get. Almost inevitably something will happen; your job is to catch it when it does.

Example: Leaving a Job

For instance, Nancy wanted to quit her job at Stanford University and go into consulting full time. But every time she thought of giving up that secure and regular paycheck she would feel anxious and depressed, and would think up some reason or another to postpone her decision for an additional month. She attended one of our workshops, and quickly saw the vicious circle that had her trapped. One of the reprogramming strategies she chose to try was exaggeration. Over the course of about six weeks she used it effectively and, in conjunction with other tools, was successful in breaking free. She now consults full time. Here is a brief sample of the exaggeration work she did.

Giving herself half an hour or so to work, Nancy sat down and clearly imagined resigning from Stanford. Rather than fighting the anxiety and sadness as it began to rise, she opened herself to it, focused inward, and asked "Specifically, what is scary or sad about leaving Stanford?" She flashed on a mental image of the paycheck she wouldn't be getting, and imagined not being able to make it financially on her own. She saw the faces of two women who worked in her office, suddenly saw herself sitting alone in a cold barren private office in a huge industrial park. Strangely, she imagined herself arriving at work and entering the office to find the coffee pot empty and cold. With this image her sadness deepened. She continued to sit quietly imagining she was on her own, allowing the images and feelings to arise, intensify, and change as they would, while paying careful attention to everything. Then she began to exaggerate.

Nancy told herself, "Kiddo, you can't make it on your own! You'll be lonely!" She visualized the office even starker and colder than before, with no furniture except for a metal desk and a single chair. "You'll fail, and then what will you do?" She then imagined herself calling her ex-husband for money; her anxiety level jumped and she felt a surge of anger. "And you'll never find a man sitting out there all alone! At least at Stanford there are some guys around. You'll have to go back to him . . ." (visualizing her ex) ". . . or grow old alone . . ." (and visualized herself grey-haired, arthritic, and fat, sitting in her office in front of that bare metal desk).

Nancy continued to freely associate to the worst-possible fantasies that came up. When out of new material, she simply reran an old sequence that seemed to have some emotional effect. Or she simply made up a new one to see what would happen. At certain points she reported that some of the fantasies almost seemed real, and she truly became afraid. At such times it was hard to keep going, but she did. (Never stop in the middle of a duplication process. Don't reassure yourself, or do anything else that will help you avoid. Once started, continue working until the intensity of your negative emotion begins to come down on its own.) At such times she would use the added fear and sense of reality to help her exaggerate, saying to herself, "See? You're right! You really can't make it in the real world! It's true! All you're good for is a damn cloistered school!" And she would see herself crawling back and begging to be kept on at Stanford.

At some point in the exaggeration session, Nancy would begin to feel bored, and lose the ability to frighten herself by thinking up new worst-possibles. Her nervousness would ease; at that point she would terminate the session.

Gradually a different flavor began to creep into her work. For one thing, memories began to appear. Some of these seemed to have no relevance to the Stanford/job issue, while others were obviously related. For instance, one day she recalled that her mother used to sit at a small metal desk and write long letters to her father during the years he spent fighting in Korea. With that image her feelings of loneliness and depression intensified, and one more piece of the puzzle was in place. She worked with these images as she had with the various other trigger elements she'd found.

Eventually Nancy began to see what she called "graveyard humor" in the barrier systems. Someone in her workshop had told her of the "golden handcuff" metaphor ("I'd like to leave my job but they pay me too well," and variations thereof). She saw herself as a withered skeleton, hundreds of years in the future, complete with cobwebs, still seated at her little wooden desk at Stanford—fastened forever to one of its legs with great, shining chains. Other images, such as the metal desk and single chair in the bare room became funny to her as well. Of course, the ability to see the humorous side of one's own predicament is a very good sign. Nancy's worst-possibles soon became manageable, and she was able to make a decision about her job.

Quite a number of behaviorally-oriented therapists use exaggeration strategies in their clinical work. Some use them for duplication purposes, others to create a humorous effect; and still others as paradox to prompt clients into making some change. And many also prescribe exaggeration as homework, believing that it is an effective self-help strategy as well. For instance, a man who was afraid to fall asleep with the radio on, for fear he would be electrocuted or burned to death, was told to lie in bed listening to the radio and exaggerate those fears until he fell asleep. Insomniacs are often told to spend the night exaggerating wakefulness: to stare at the ceiling with eyes wide open and try as hard as possible not to sleep a wink. Although we would not use this particular approach, some programs to help people stop smoking begin by a kind of exaggeration procedure. The participants are told to smoke cigarette after cigarette, as fast as they can, pack after pack, for several hours, until they begin to feel sick at the very thought of a cigarette. Often such a tactic will give the participants a day or two head start on the program before their nicotine fits return.

To summarize, exaggeration is an optional duplication tactic meant to help you intensify feelings, behaviors or negative fantasies. Exaggeration sometimes helps speed up the reprogramming process and may aid in recovering related semiconscious material.

STEP 5:   **If a clearer memory, image, voice or other internal experience suddenly appears during duplication, work with it, even if it seems totally unrelated to the subject at hand.**

As mentioned, the intensity of certain duplication processes sometimes brings memories and other repressed material into consciousness. If you have such an experience, pay attention to it! It may prove to be of little value; but much more often we've found that sudden flashes of memory or awareness during duplication are of critical significance in the barrier system as a whole.

Precisely what to do with these recalled experiences depends on the situation at hand. However, it's often valuable to stop working on the original pattern and try to clarify, duplicate, or exaggerate the new material in some way. If you try this and you suddenly become more emotional, you're probably on the right track. Then, when you've brought that cycle to a close, return to your original task. Often you will find that your job has been simplified considerably and reprogramming can be completed more quickly than otherwise would have been possible.

STEP 6:   End the process with a positive experience. DON'T STOP IN THE MIDDLE!

All your reprogramming processes should be ended with a "smile"; this is particularly true with regard to duplication. The duplication process can be an exhilarating experience, but it also can be painful, tedious, frightening, and sometimes embarrassing. So you deserve a reward at the end of it. Also, the process itself will work a lot better if you end it on a positive note. When you have been duplicating a target behavior, ending on a positive note means doing something fun, rewarding, or pleasant before calling it a day. Go for a jog (if that's fun for you), an ice cream (if you're not on a diet!), or treat yourself to a little of something you like to do.

If you're duplicating feeling patterns, ending on a positive note means ending while the negative feeling is decreasing. And then give yourself a treat of some kind.

What do you do if you've been working for awhile, and need to stop, and the negatives are not decreasing? This probably means that you've been working with too general a target situation or set of worst-possibles. Let go of everything except one specific, concrete, minor target element and work with that until your feelings begin to lighten. Or, as a last resort, return to an element that you've already worked through once or twice, and know that you can deal with fairly easily. If you find yourself out of time, and you have to go to work or your parents are coming over or you have to sing at the Glee Club recital in fifteen minutes and you need to slap an emotional bandaid on everything for awhile, then do it. Nothing horrible will happen to you. Stop where you have to stop, shove everything back under the rug, and leave for work or whatever. But come back and finish the job as quickly as you can. Remember that the basic purpose of duplication is to help you break avoidance patterns that are keeping you from reaching your goals. If you end every session by pasting yourself back together with avoidance strategies, the procedure won't work. Go out for roller derby instead. It's healthier aerobically, no more painful, and you'll still get to go around in a circle as fast as you can.

When working with negative anticipations, end at a point when the worst-possible you've been running somehow seems less important or serious, or you begin to see the humor in the silly thing. Then run a *best*-possible fantasy, just once, but pulling out all the stops as you do.

And most important of all, it's warm fuzzy time! Spend a few moments honoring yourself for being willing to choose to go through pain, anxiety, embarrassment, or tedium in order to change and grow. Remember, there's still a part inside you that believes that the barrier system you've been trying to dissolve is operating in your best interest—or at least was once set up to serve you. That part of you has agreed to help you reprogram (we hope!), but probably retains some doubts about the whole thing. So give that part special attention: he or she deserves it.

Prevention Strategies

In Chapter 1 of Aldous Huxley's *Island*, a young man is shipwrecked at the base of a towering cliff on a moonless night. Barely able to see his hands in front of his face, he begins to scale the cliff. Halfway to the top, dead tired and drenched with spray, he pauses to rest. He can barely find toe-holds on the cliff, he can't see at all, and faces certain death if he falls. Then he realizes that the few ledges on the cliff face are completely covered with snakes! His terror and revulsion are so intense that he nearly falls back, choosing death over the horror of his surroundings. But he climbs on, and finally collapses, unconscious, on a grassy plateau above the cliff.

The next morning he awakens to find a young girl staring down at him. She asks, "Did you climb up over the cliff of snakes?"

Her words bring memories of the night before crashing down around him; he closes his eyes and begins to shudder. She kneels by his side, and touches him on the shoulder. "Let me help you," she commands. "If you don't heal your memories of last night, you'll carry their scars for life." And systematically, almost cruelly, she makes the young man relive his dreadful climb of the night before. Each time in greater detail, she has him imagine it and describe it to her. At first, it brings up hidden terrors he didn't even know were there, and he begs her to stop. But she persists, and finally he is able to imagine his climb with little emotional reaction. At that point she rises, and says "Now I will take you to meet my father." She turns her back and walks away.

A most interesting and provocative way to begin a

novel. Obviously Huxley wanted his readers to wonder just what sort of people inhabited this remote and uncharted island and what other strange rites and customs they practiced. Were they a race of wandering sadists who liked nothing more than rubbing one another's noses in the memories of horrible experiences? Maybe they all went stranger-baiting on Sunday afternoons. Or did they possess a deeper and possibly much clearer understanding of the workings of the human mind than most "modern" cultures do? Did Huxley's young island girl indeed save her shipwrecked visitor from the lasting consequences of a traumatic and deeply disturbing experience? We have no way of knowing for certain. But if you've read this far, our biases on the matter ought to be clear by now.

We believe the island girl may have done her visitor a great favor when she helped him duplicate his memories of the night before. And, though *Island* is fiction, the technique Huxley described is as practical as hanging a fire extinguisher in the kitchen. Phobias, like fires, can be nipped in the bud. All it takes is good timing, a knowledge of what to do, and the willingness to do it. Unfortunately most of us don't have strange girls hanging around waiting to assist us every time we've been seriously upset by something. So if we, our clients, and our loved ones are to benefit from the power of "preventative duplication," we shall have to learn to do it ourselves.

Opportunities to use duplication arise a lot more often than you might think. Minor everyday occurrences which alone wouldn't have much lasting impact, no matter how they were handled, add up. Barrier patterns are thus developed gradually, outside of awareness and over a period of time. The problem is that few of us have

been trained to recognize the opportunities, or would
know what to do if we did recognize them. Instead we've
learned to use explanation, reassurance, rationalization,
sympathy and various other tactics to help us and those we
serve avoid the "snakes."

Three-year-old Johnny is frightened by the neighbor's cat and breaks into tears. His mother says, "Aw,
don't cry, honey. That ol' cat didn't really hurt you, did
he? Come on, dry your eyes; there's mommy's little man."
Pretty soon Johnny stops crying. But is he truly reassured? We doubt it. Here he is, upset because a huge
beast nearly ripped his face off, and his mother tells him
(indirectly) that he is wrong to cry and that not crying will
make him a man. Imagine Huxley's island girl saying,
"Don't worry about it, Mister. The snakes on the cliff
didn't hurt you, did they? C'mon, be a man. Stop shaking
and I might let you kiss me."

We might suggest, instead, that Johnny's mother
hold her son in her arms and say, "Wow, that ol' kitty
really surprised you, didn't he? You go ahead and cry loud!
My goodness, what a big strong voice you have!" First,
she makes it perfectly all right for Johnny to cry. Then,
from within a context of acceptance and love, she begins to
direct his attention to a part of the experience that he can
feel good about. But never does she tell Johnny to change
anything, nor suggest that any part of his experience is bad
or wrong. Instead, she supports her son and (of course)
stays with him if she possibly can until he stops crying on
his own.

Similarly, we had a client whose daughter was
plagued with dreams of wolves coming through her bed-

room window to attack her. She refused to discuss the dreams during the day, but at night often fled her room in tears, demanding that her mother sit with her until she fell asleep. The mother had tried every device she could think of to reassure her daughter about wolves, but to no avail. Nothing would help but that she sat up with her daughter at night. The mother was bright enough to realize that at some level she was rewarding the very fears and behaviors she wished to eliminate, but didn't know what else to do.

We instructed Mom in the gentle art of duplication, gave her some practice in the office, and then sent her home to try it out. She returned the next week grinning from ear to ear, and carrying a couple of tapes she'd made. Here is some sample dialogue between mother and daughter, taken from the middle portions of one tape:

Mother: "I don't know about anybody else, but I'd be scared if I thought wolves were coming in my window!"

Kathy: (Sniffing, sounding a little perplexed) "Yeah . . ."

M: "Kathy, what do you think these wolves are going to do to you?"

K: "They're going to hurt me. Eat me up."

M: "Gee, Kath, what do you think they might start with?"

K: "What?"

M: "Where do you think they might start eating? On your leg, right here? I might start there if I were a wolf!"

K: (Wails) "Yes! And on my arms and my stomach!" (Then, emphatically, but without tears) "They'd eat me up!"

M: (Just as emphatically) "I know, honey, and then where would you be, you'd be all gone . . ."

K: (Interrupting) "In the wolf's tummy!"

M: "That sure would be a full wolf! He better watch it, he might get a tummyache."

K: "Yeah!"

M: "Then he might have to lie down and take a nap."

K: "He'd lie down in that corner over there."

M: "Well he better not go potty on the floor, that's all I can say."

K: "Mommy, now you're being silly!"

M: "I don't know, sounds like a pretty scary dream to me. Which window do you think he might come in?" (And she takes Kathy back through the dream/fantasy experience again. By the end of the tape both are laughing.)

Space limitations prevent us from giving a detailed analysis of this sort of strategy and its long-term effects. However, we might briefly deal with a few worst-possible fantasies certain readers may be having at this point.

1. The time and attention Kathy's mother devoted to the content of her child's dream will not leave Kathy with permanent wolf nightmares. Reinforcement doesn't work that way.

2. Kathy will not become emotionally crippled from having to face the fantasy of being eaten by a wolf. She might, however, if she spends the rest of her life running away from such a fantasy.

3. Mom will not have to spend every night for the next fifteen years coming up with more and more creative dream fantasies. After helping her deal with irrational fears, however, she might consider teaching Kathy more appropriate ways to get attention.

4. The wolf was not Kathy's father's penis in disguise. Or maybe it was, who knows? Either way, we doubt if it matters very much.

To summarize, a young mother helped her daughter to face her own particular brand of "snake." She did so by leading Kathy through related and exaggerated experiences again and again. She always respected and accepted what Kathy felt, said, and did as "right"; was never flip, casual, or sarcastic; never left Kathy when she was still badly frightened; and operated from a position of love and warmth.*

Finally, she helped Kathy see the humorous side of her dreams and the fears they produced, helped her see the funny side of the whole thing (when possible). Which brings us to the final issue to be dealt with in this chapter: the art of the cosmic chuckle.**

The Art of the Cosmic Chuckle

Our friend and colleague Deane Shapiro first introduced us to the phrase, "cosmic chuckle." In a book that compares Eastern and Western self-control strategies, Deane writes, "On the one hand, a jolt is a crisis. On the other side, it is part of what might be called the cosmic chuckle—the ability to stand back and observe the events of one's life with humor: both the wry humor which acknowledges the absurdity of life and the joyous, happy humor which recognizes its grandeur and beauty." Finding the cosmic chuckle means, among other things, trans-

*We cannot overemphasize the importance of doing this and any duplication procedure within a context of acceptance, warmth, and love; and with a clear intention to assist. Duplication is not a carte blanche invitation to passive aggression in the name of love, or to scare your kid half to death because he or she woke you up in the middle of the night with a bad dream.

**We do not mean to imply here that parents should be able to help their kids with all the fears and irrational beliefs that are a part of childhood. If your child has an emotional problem, we strongly suggest that you seek professional help.

cending the "Either-Or" fallacy once and for all. Being able to take yourself seriously and laugh at yourself simultaneously. A most valuable—and elusive—skill.

On a practical level the cosmic chuckle seems to be a kind of ultimate duplication tactic. After you practice duplication skills for a while they begin to become a way of life. You begin to employ them spontaneously, without really having to think about it. Gradually, the automatic avoidance reactions you learned over the years begin to fade; you confront, duplicate, and discharge negative experiences as they happen. You begin to pay more attention to life experiences even as you let go of your need to experience life in a particular fashion. Generally, you make better choices as a result.

Eventually you begin to take "serious" matters less seriously. You see the humorous angle that is embedded in all "crisis" situations because it is so fundamentally a part of the human condition itself. The cosmic chuckle is the ultimate duplication, the ability to laugh at oneself—to dance, if necessary, with Zorba, in the very rubble of one's dreams. We suggest that you nurture your own version of the cosmic chuckle even as you work hard on the various strategies outlined in this book. Develop it, cherish it, let it flower; it may be the greatest healer of them all.

SUMMARY

Duplication is one of the oldest and most widely-used self-help strategies known to man. Since the time of Aristotle, people have been using duplication in one form or another to treat every kind of problem from stuttering to psychosis.

Tactically, duplication is a straightforward procedure to use. First, specify a feeling or behavior that you would like to change. Then define the precise conditions (or triggers) under which the feeling or behavior occurs. Third, in one way or another expose yourself to the conditions that seem to trigger that feeling or behavior you'd like to reprogram.

If you're working on a behavior, voluntarily practice that behavior in the face of the trigger conditions that would cause it to occur. If possible, exaggerate the target behavior. Repeat this process over and over until the behavior is under your conscious control—that is, until it no longer occurs automatically under the trigger conditions you've specified.

If you're working on a feeling, exaggerate whatever cues bring out that feeling. For instance, if you're afraid to fly, imagine as graphically as you can that you're on an airplane that's about to crash. If you can get yourself to do it, actually take an airplane flight. During the flight, make yourself pay attention to all the cues that frighten you: the sound of the landing gear being lowered, the sight of the crack in the wing outside your window, the feeling of turbulence, and so on.

The human animal is infinitely skilled at avoiding discomfort whenever possible. Choosing to focus on anxiety-producing triggers may be more difficult than you think. But if you're able to do so and to practice repeatedly and systematically according to the principles outlined in this chapter, your anxieties will eventually begin to fade.

Generally, chronic and long-standing feelings and behaviors are much more difficult to reprogram than are relatively new patterns. If you can catch an unwanted behavior pattern or emotional reaction early on, the re-programming process usually will not take very long. In this way duplication can serve as a preventative measure as well as a therapeutic one: if you can work on the problem while it's forming, early intervention may literally save you years of crippling discomfort.

When you first begin the duplication process, your negative feelings will probably get worse for awhile. This is natural; don't panic! And above all, don't stop in the middle of a duplication exercise: continue the procedure until you begin to feel better despite your attempts to make yourself feel worse. Bailing out in the middle of an exercise may only serve to strengthen the negative feelings and behavior patterns you've been trying to shed.

7

Emotional Reprogramming

In this chapter we will describe a technique that combines the association and sequencing procedures you learned in Chapter 5 with the duplication tactics presented in Chapter 6. This is a procedure designed specifically to help you deal with negative feelings after you've already become upset.

Up till now, we've suggested that you do your reprogramming in advance, in order to help you deal with difficult situations when they do occur. But real life can be surprising. We can't program out all our emotional sensitivity (nor would we want to!), and we can't prepare for every possible situation that might occur. So we need a set of techniques that can be used "after the fact." Something that will come in handy when we've already been blindsided, our biocomputers have gone on automatic, and we're about to lose control.

That's where emotional reprogramming comes in. Emotional reprogramming is designed to diffuse negative feelings, and use the energy embedded in those feelings to help replace negative images and self-statements with positive ones. This occurs in two ways:

1. The reprogramming process provides a vehicle for the expression of intense negative emotion. According to the therapeutic principle of catharsis, the direct expression of a bothersome feeling may help to reduce the intensity of that feeling. In emotional reprogramming, the trainee duplicates whatever negative emotions he or she may be having. Then, through systematic exaggeration and repetition, these feelings can be reduced or eliminated, according to principles described in Chapter 6.

2. When upset, most people tend to say negative things to themselves. Unfortunately, this is just the time they most need caring and support. In emotional reprogramming, the trainee learns to associate positive, rather than negative, self-statements to the negative emotions he or she is experiencing. Eventually, these negative feelings will automatically trigger the positive self-statements. That is, the trainee will learn to respond to anger, fear, or disappointment with self-support and a reasonable optimism, rather than with self-talk that leads to a pessimistic viewpoint.

Here is an example of how emotional reprogramming works. Joanne's husband, Andy, is an hour and a half late for dinner. Joanne is angry that Andy neither came home when expected, nor called to say that he would be late. If this had happened a year ago, her back and stomach would have been tense and her head splitting with pain. She would have slammed around the kitchen, mumbling, "If that bastard loved me, he wouldn't treat me like this! I ought to throw his dinner right in his face! Why couldn't I have found somebody who would treat me decently?" And in her mind's eye, of course, Joanne would have imagined Andy at every bar, flirting with every cocktail waitress between the office and home.

But Joanne has been trained in emotional reprogramming. So she takes her growing annoyance and jealousy into the bedroom, and spends fifteen minutes dealing with the emotions she knows will ruin her evening if she lets them. When she emerges, her body is relaxed and she's in a somewhat better mood. She thinks of Andy stopping for a drink on the way home, and says to herself with a shrug, "Well, I hope he's on his way home, and I do wish he'd called. But I can have a good evening even if I have to eat alone. I can feel good about myself even when Andy breaks an agreement with me." Mind you, Joanne retains a strong preference that Andy show up when he says he will. And she may tell him that in no uncertain terms when he does come in. But she no longer has to ruin her evening over the fact that he's late.

PROCEDURES

The steps laid out in this section represent but one of many variations on emotional reprogramming we've found useful with our clients and trainees. We suggest you practice the process as we've outlined it here. After you become familiar with its effects, you may streamline it or adopt whatever variations may better fit your individual needs. In the next section, we'll describe a variation suited to people who might prefer to work more quietly. As before, a worksheet is provided at the end of the chapter.*

STEP 1: Ask yourself, "Specifically, what is happening to upset me?" That is, define the source of your upset as specifically as you can.

As we mentioned earlier, these procedures are to be used when you are actively upset. Use emotional reprogramming when your husband is late for dinner and you're fuming; when the neighborhood superstar has just put a softball through your new stained-glass window; when an attractive woman at the singles club has just turned you down out-of-hand. In theory, the more intense the emotion, the better the technique will work.

Define *precisely* what is upsetting you. Use the specification skills you learned in Chapter 2. You may be feeling angry and a little frightened because your husband is two months late with the alimony payments. Exactly what is it that you are imagining, visualizing, or anticipating that is upsetting you so?

Are you imagining your ex at the amusement park with another woman, while you're struggling to make ends meet? Are you visualizing your bank balance, and thinking that if he misses a third payment you're going to have to apply for welfare? You may then picture, in your mind's eye, the disapproving looks on the faces of your parents.

Often a variety of images are associated with the overall situation that is making you unhappy. Specify as many of these images as you can.

*This particular programming variation was adapted from the work of Ken Keyes.

STEP 2: Take full responsibility for "creating" your own upset feelings.

We believe that this step is absolutely critical to the success of the emotional reprogramming process. Intellectually, most people are willing to admit that they are at least partially responsible for upsetting themselves under certain circumstances. But when the chips are down and emotion is up, the philosophy goes out the window and blame is very quickly directed outward. A very human reaction—but completely contradictory to the goals of emotional reprogramming.

As Epictetus, the Greek philosopher, once said: "Men are disturbed not by things, but by the views which they take of them." It is the *meaning* that we put on events that upsets us, not the events themselves. For instance, there is nothing intrinsically upsetting about Andy's being late coming home from the office. He may have had a lot of work to do. And he may have tried to call, but been unable to get through—or possibly he simply forgot.

Rather, it's Joanne's interpretation of what happened that upsets her. She imagines Andy stopping at the corner bar and flirting with the cocktail waitresses. She says to herself, "If he respected me the way a husband should, he wouldn't treat me like this." She imagines he's having an affair on the side, or visualizes a fatal traffic accident. Either way, she thinks to herself, "My God! I'm going to be alone . . ." and so on.

Andy may be wrong to be late. It simply doesn't do Joanne any good to criticize him *in absentia* and then spend the better part of an evening feeling bad about her husband, her marriage, and herself. Much better to spend a

reasonably pleasant evening, and then (should she choose
to) roundly criticize her husband when he arrives home.

In any event, take responsibility for creating the
images and self-statements that in turn create the feelings
you wish to reprogram. It may take a little willpower to let
the person or situation involved "off the hook"—but
emotional reprogramming will be much less effective if
you don't. Hanging onto the unfairness of it all, or onto
the rightness of your position, will simply serve to reinforce your pain.

STEP 3:   **Specify one or more "demands" that you are
              making of the person or the situation in-
              volved. Using pencil and paper, write one or
              more statements of the form, "I (upset my-
              self) by demanding that (unfulfilled need)."**

We upset ourselves when we feel our needs aren't
being met. Generally speaking, these upset-producing
needs can be couched in the form of "demand statements." Here are a few examples.

"I make myself angry by demanding that Andy call
me from the office if he's going to be late."

"I make myself frightened by demanding that
women accept my invitations to dinner." (This from a shy
young man at a singles club.)

"I make myself depressed by demanding that my
IBM stock go up." (An investor feeling bad about recent
declines in his portfolio.)

This is a very straight-forward step. In order to stay
out of trouble, we suggest that you stick as closely as you
can to the demand statement format given above.
Remember, the purpose of the demand statement is to

specify, in concrete terms, the manner in which you are responsible for producing and maintaining the negative feelings in question. Anything you use which is true to that intent will work whether it follows the above format or not.

On the other hand, it's possible to follow the format and still cheat. Some time ago we worked with a mother who became enraged when her teenage daughter didn't follow certain rules her mother had set, or otherwise behaved in ways with which her mother disagreed. When we asked her to generate some demand statements, these are two she came up with.

"I make myself angry by demanding that Marlene do the right thing at home."

"I make myself upset by demanding that my daughter clean her room the way she should."

Both these statements are absolutely correct in form. But they still declare that Marlene's mother is right to be angry with her daughter. As we said before, she may be right. But the need to proclaim it, to stick openly to that position, will slow down the process of emotional reprogramming and make it more difficult for Mother to give up her anger.

STEP 4: Formulate one or more "reprogramming statements." Use the following form: "I can (positive feeling statement) when (demand isn't met)."

Here are some examples of reprogramming statements.

"I can feel good about myself when John doesn't come on time for dinner."

"I can enjoy myself and this racquetball game even when I miss an easy shot."

"I can feel like a good mother even when Marlene stays out till 3 a.m."

Each of these statements is in the form of what we might call a "letting-go affirmation." Note the differences between letting-go affirmations and the type of statements traditionally employed in sales training classes and personal growth seminars which employ the power of positive thinking. One of the oldest and most famous of these may be paraphrased, "Every day, in every way, I can feel myself getting better and better."* Among others, Napoleon Hill used this form in his "Greatest Salesman in the World" classes and Jose Silva in his Silva Mind Control seminars. The "every day in every way" affirmation form has value. However, in emotional reprogramming we suggest that you employ the letting-go form instead.

Essentially, a letting-go affirmation is one which affirms your "OK-ness" at a time when you would normally feel badly about yourself. As we discussed, people generally feel upset when their needs, which they have translated into demands, aren't met. As you will see, letting-go affirmations can be used to form a kind of positive bridge between feelings and demands.

When we don't think we are going to get what we want, most of us commit a variation of the Either-Or fallacy (see Chapter 8). Specifically, we say to ourselves, "Either I get what I want (have my demand met) or I get upset. Letting-go affirmations provide a clear third alternative to the Either-Or position. In the examples below,

---

*To our knowledge statements of this type were first used in the late 19th century as self-hypnosis tools by Emil Coué.

the left-hand column contains an either-or statement (note that an either-or statement may appear in various forms); the right-hand column contains a third alternative statement, framed in the form of a letting-go affirmation.

Either I win the tennis game or I've wasted my afternoon.	I can lose the game and still have a perfectly enjoyable day.
If I stutter on stage, no one will like my talk.	I can stutter on stage and still give a good speech.
Either Marlene does exactly what I say or it proves I'm a terrible mother.	I can feel good about myself as a mother even when Marlene disobeys me.
I must be worthless. Andy doesn't even care enough to call.	I can love myself and feel good even when Andy doesn't call.
They've asked me to retire. If I can't work, my life is meaningless.	I can respect myself and have a rich, meaningful life when I retire early.

Needs vs. Preference

How would you define the difference between a "need" and a "preference"? Initially, quite a few of our trainees think the difference is mainly a matter of degree. For instance, a need for a long-term relationship would be defined as stronger or more intense than a preference for a long-term relationship.

But there are big differences between needs and preferences. Certainly if we believe we have a strong need we feel and behave differently than if we believe we have a strong preference. An unfulfilled need implies suffering. A need filled implies a return to the status quo. On the other hand, if a preference goes unfulfilled there may be disappointment, but no real loss. If a preference is satisfied, happiness or pleasure will result.

Needs are often connected with the idea of survival itself. That is, we believe at some level that if our needs are not met we may die (physically, psychologically, or emotionally). Preferences have nothing to do with survival. We may be disappointed if they are not fulfilled, and when the preferences are strong we may be very disappointed indeed, but we know we can make it anyway; we know we will not die. No matter how strong our preferences may be they do not bind us—we are still free. Thus, Woody strongly prefers that his wife not sleep with another man. If she does he may be sad, disappointed, frightened of losing her—and eventually he may choose to terminate the marriage as a result. But no matter what he does, Woody knows he will be able to make it on his own if he has to. Todd, on the other hand, needs his wife to be faithful. Her sleeping with another man would threaten the survival of his male ego, his feelings of self-worth as a human being, and possibly his very life. And Todd may well say to himself, "I just couldn't handle Martha being unfaithful to me; I just couldn't go on." In other words, "If my need for her fidelity isn't met, I may die."

At any rate, *the purpose of emotional reprogramming is to help you change needs to preferences.* Needs, when they are not real, physical needs, are supported by belief systems which are simply wrong. Sometimes these belief systems can be attacked rationally; but as we said earlier, belief barriers are often highly resistant to change. Emotional reprogramming can sometimes serve to dissolve the structure of the barrier system that helps maintain the irrational mind-belief. When that can be done, the belief system, and thus the need, gradually melt away leaving but a preference in their place. This is reprogramming in the purest sense of the word. It is based on repetitive, focused procedures that work on the structure rather than on the content of the belief system.

STEP 5: Sit or kneel in front of a large pillow or other soft object. Visualize the experiences, fantasies, and other images associated with your negative feelings. Clarify and intensify those images in order to exaggerate their emotional effect. Intensify the upset feelings as much as possible. As the feelings build, repeat your demand statement, over and over, as loudly as you can. Yell it, shout it out. If you wish, express yourself physically by pounding on the pillow in front of you. Continue to focus on the upsetting images, and repeat your demand statement, until nothing you do makes the feelings worse.

Your job at this stage is to duplicate and intensify the negative feelings you wish to reprogram. Exaggerate them as much as you can. Continue pounding, yelling your demand statement, and focusing on the upsetting images until your feelings peak. When your upset feelings are no longer getting worse, move on to Step 6.

As we've said, there may be a considerable cathartic value in this stage of the exercise. The value in and the rationale behind duplicating unwanted behavior patterns was discussed in the last chapter. But in addition, this step will prepare you to "install" the reprogramming statements you constructed earlier.

Human beings seem to be most sensitized to certain kinds of learning when they're upset. (This doesn't mean you should get angry in order to learn Spanish. The conscious memory function seems to be inhibited by intense emotion in most people.) For example, researchers have shown that, under the proper circumstances, individuals can be helped to recall intensely emotional experiences (e.g., traumas) with almost photographic accuracy.*

It would seem, then, that if they're handled right, upsetting experiences could actually be used as opportunities for learning. It is upon this idea that the procedures of emotional reprogramming are based.

STEP 6: When the upsetting feelings have peaked, when you can no longer intensify them, substitute your reprogramming statement for your demand statement. Continue to focus on and exaggerate the negative images. Continue to pound the pillow in front of you. Say/shout/scream your reprogramming sentence at the same level of intensity you did your demand statement. Continue until, no matter what you do, the negative feelings begin to recede. They need not disappear entirely, however you must continue repro-

---

*Virginia Johnson at UCLA has used hypnotic procedures to duplicate traumatic conditions in research subjects. She has shown, for instance, that the victims of traffic accidents can literally recall the numbers on the license plates of cars that hit them.

gramming until you are certain they have become less intense.

In this step you are literally using the intensity of your negative feelings to program in, or "install," positive self-statements to take the place of the negative statements and images generally associated with feeling badly. This is the sequencing portion of the program. Eventually, the negative feelings you experience will automatically trigger letting-go affirmations, just as they now trigger self-criticism and other negative material. The immediate purpose of this exercise, of course, is to help you deal with the particular upset that's bothering you now. But with diligent practice, the need to use this technique at all (except under extraordinary circumstances) will begin to fade. When negative feelings lead automatically to positive statements instead of negative ones, the deadly thought-feeling-thought-feeling vicious circles that plague so many millions of people will cease to be a problem for you. It will take awhile, but when it happens, what a fine outcome that will be!

Remember, don't stop reprogramming until your negative feelings become significantly less intense and continue to decrease no matter what you do to intensify them. We've found that the absolute level of feeling intensity is less important an indicator than is the direction of change. That is, move on to Step 7 when you can feel yourself becoming less upset, even though a certain amount of upset may still be present.

STEP 6A: If, during Step 6, you find yourself getting more upset, continue reprogramming. If you realize that new upsetting images have

arisen, return to Step 4 and use these new
images to produce additional demand
statements. Then, move to Step 5 and continue as before.

Occasionally the reprogramming process will stimu-
late additional memories, anticipations, or other upsetting
images. If new material comes up for you, reprogram it!
Don't try to ignore it just because you're supposed to be
working on the old material. In the fantasy game, it is
important to pay careful attention and take what you get.
At each moment during Steps 5 and 6 you should be
focusing on and working with whatever images are most
upsetting to you now.

On the other hand, don't jump around on purpose. If
you can focus on one specific upsetting image at a time,
then do it. If you're like most people, you have years and
years of negative material stored up inside you some-
where. You don't have to reprogram it all in one sitting!
Remember the old joke about how to eat an elephant?
Well, reprogramming works best when you can do it the
same way: one bite at a time.

STEP 7:   Relax and allow your mind and body to be
          calm for a moment. Then close your eyes
          and focus once more on the upsetting ex-
          perience. Pay careful attention to your reac-
          tions. If you still feel upset, return to Step 5
          and complete another reprogramming cycle.
          If the negative feelings have substantially
          lessened or disappeared, congratulations!
          Give yourself a mental hug, you deserve it.

In practice, it's often necessary to cycle through Steps 5-7 several times before the negative feelings cease to return. There's no right number of times to reprogram. After you complete each cycle, take a deep breath, close your eyes, and quietly pay attention to whether or not you're still upset. If you are, run Steps 5-7 again.

Often it's impossible to get rid of the negative emotion completely. But when the reprogramming has worked you'll know it. There will be a definite change in the quality as well as the amount of the upset you feel. It will be as if the emotion, while still there, is no longer so bothersome—is no longer controlling you. Remember your demand statement; no doubt you will still have a preference that the demand be met. But the irrational, controlling need that it be met will be gone. Your preference may still be strong. But you, rather than it, will now be in the driver's seat.

Spontaneous Recovery and Generalization

Unfortunately, the negative feelings will probably come back. As mentioned elsewhere in this book, long-standing habit patterns often "spontaneously recover" after reprogramming. When your need is a deep-seated one and the accompanying belief system has been with you for years, its elements must usually be reprogrammed many times before the pattern as a whole begins to fade. Remember, spontaneous recovery is a natural phenomenon. Stick to your reprogramming. Eventually the negative feelings will "extinguish" for good, and will bother you no more (unless they're brought on by something else).

A word of caution. During Step 8 evaluate only the emotion-related images that you worked on during reprogramming. Some trainees have a tendency to look for sensitivity to any thought or image which could possibly cause a negative reaction. Usually they find some, get upset again, and have more reprogramming to do (or become confused and feel that they have failed). Remember, you don't have to do it all at one sitting. Limit your internal check to the specific images and demand statements you've been using during Steps 5 and 6. Try not to think of anything else at all. Separate those particular images from the complex underlying problem and try to treat them as completely independent items. This is not always easy to do and sometimes associations will occur spontaneously but, as we mentioned earlier, work on one specific element at a time if possible.

On the positive side of generalization, it is also rarely necessary to reprogram an underlying problem exhaustively. For instance, Susan's relationship with her rebellious daughter Marlene is complicated and contains literally hundreds of charged issues. But Susan won't have to work on each one individually before she ceases to grind her teeth every time Marlene comes home from school. After she's reprogrammed twenty or thirty emotional reactions, always working on the ones that occur naturally in the course of her daily life, her sensitivity to her daughter's behavior in general will begin to fade. The relationship itself may well begin to change, as Marlene begins to notice her mother reacting differently. The specific trigger situations Susan will work on over the months are a little like bricks in a wall. Knock out a few bricks and the wall gets weaker. Knock out a couple more, and the whole thing falls down. It's not necessary to deal with each brick individually. And neither do you have to push the wall over all at once. The best strategy is to get your mallet and chisel, pick one individual brick, and get to work.

Don't Stop in the Middle

Before moving on, a word of caution about the emotional reprogramming process. The techniques involved are powerful, and they work. Sometimes intense emotions are involved and trainees are reluctant to attempt the process on their own. If you feel at all nervous about using emotional reprogramming by yourself, then please don't do it! Find someone to help you, or seek professional assistance. Alternatively, it's perfectly permissible to have a trusted friend sit quietly by while you work. As we mentioned in Chapter 6, the establishment of a safe, positive, context that you trust is a vital part of any reprogramming process.

Reasonably, we believe there are people who should not use this variation of emotional reprogramming, and have described an alternative strategy at the end of the chapter. If you're uncertain about yourself, please use the tension-release method described on page 190. However, both authors have used the emotive variant described above with a wide variety of clinical and "neurotic normal" populations, and experienced no negative effects of any kind (aside from a bit of hoarseness here and there).

As far as we know there is only one significant way in which the emotional reprogramming process can be counterproductive. And that is if you stop in the middle. Some people begin the procedure, crank the intensity up to 9, and then get frightened of their own feelings and want to pull back. DON'T STOP IN THE MIDDLE! Once you've begun the emotive portion of the process (Step 5), continue until your reaction peaks and begins to come down of its own accord. That is, keep trying to make it worse until it begins to lessen no matter what you do to keep it at the peak level. If you get frightened in the middle of Step 5, decide you want to stop, and then proceed to reduce the emotional intensity with some kind of avoidance maneuver (trying to think of something else, reassuring yourself, yelling at the kids, whatever), it's possible you'll wind up sensitized rather than desensitized to the images and demand statements you've been working with. So, once you start, keep going. DON'T STOP IN THE MIDDLE!

We now present an annotated example of emotional reprogramming.

Jan: Dealing with Anger and Disapointment

Jan is a bright, attractive 26-year-old woman who said she attended our workshop to learn to be more self-sufficient. Jan had recently moved to California from the Midwest, to her mother's thinly veiled disappointment, and was having some trouble adjusting to certain cultural differences on the West Coast. She knew she wanted to stay for at least a couple of years, but was having trouble meeting friends and generally feeling that she belonged. She was alternatively homesick and determined; alternatively proud of herself for making the move and despondent over the loneliness that the move had brought. A part of her, of course, wanted to move back home and be done with it. Jan's mother knew all of this, and during their frequent phone conversations she missed no opportunity to imply that her daughter should come home. She was often manipulative in her approach to the subject, and sometimes her tactics bordered on the cruel.

Jan had asked her mother a couple of times to support her in trying to build a life in California. Her mother agreed each time but quickly reverted to her former style. When she attended our workshop, Jan knew that her mother was never going to change much and that she, Jan, had to learn to be less sensitive to her mother's various ploys or break off contact entirely. Jan was unwilling to do the latter for a variety of reasons. So she decided to try emotional reprogramming instead.

As with all reprogramming procedures, when dealing with an issue as complicated as a mother-daughter relationship, it is best to pick up one or two specific, isolated situations and begin there. Also, it's best to use emotional reprogramming with "active upsets" whenever possible. So we asked Jan if there was anything currently disturbing her about her relationship with her mother, and her eyes immediately filled with tears.

It seems that Jan had sent her mother flowers on her birthday, some ten days before. When she got no call or letter in response, she checked with the florist, who told her they'd been delivered right on time. Now, more than a week later, she was feeling angry and hurt that her mother hadn't acknowledged the gift in any way. Afraid to call home, yet too angry not to call, the matter had been on Jan's mind all weekend.

The following is an annotated summary of the emotional reprogramming work we helped Jan do.

STEP 1:   Locate and specify the source of your upset.

Q1: Specifically what is upsetting you now?

A1: I sent flowers to my mother and didn't get a response. I feel angry and hurt. I see myself sending those flowers and not getting anything back, and feeling small and lonely.

Q2: Anything else directly related to that?

A2: When I think of calling my mother, I hear her voice. She sounds longsuffering. She nags me about living in California.

Q3: What might she say to you if you called her?

A3: "Honey, I'm not getting any younger, you know . . . (soft groan)." That sort of thing.

Q2: It's important to keep the reprogramming work as specific as possible. Yet, sometimes there are several internal experiences that relate directly to the upsetting situation. They will come out during reprogramming anyway, so you may as well specify them now.

STEP 2:   Take responsibility for creating and maintaining your own upset feelings.

(Jan had no trouble with this step. Intellectually, she knew that her mother was an old and

Usually, this is something you either believe or you don't. It's hard to make a conscious

lonely woman who missed her daughter and didn't know how else to communicate that to her.)

choice about it without spending time and thinking and talking about the issues involved. During this step, focus your attention upon the ways in which you create your upset feelings: what you imagine that upsets you, what you say to yourself that upsets you, etc. Then, if you still feel the other person is partly responsible for your feelings, so be it. Go ahead with the exercise, and take from it what value you can.

STEP 3:   What needs do you believe you have that are helping to create the upset? Fashion one or more demand statements out of these needs.

N1: I need my mother's approval in order to feel good about myself.

This step is usually relatively straightforward. In each case note the relationship between the demand statement and its corresponding underlying need.

D1: I make myself feel unloved by demanding my mother's approval.

N2: I need my mother's support in order to stay in San Francisco.

D2: I make myself feel insecure on the West Coast by demanding Mom's support.

N3: When I send my mother a gift, I need her response in order to feel appreciated and loved.

D3: I make myself feel un-appreciated by demanding that Mom thank me for her birthday gift.

N4: When my mother mentions her age, I feel guilty—so in order to feel good about myself, I need her not to do those things.

N4: Jan never dealt directly with her guilt feelings during this reprogramming session. Her feelings of guilt, of course, sprang from her need to feel that she was making her mother happy and not causing her mother any pain. A related demand statement might have been, "I make myself feel guilty by demanding that I keep my mother happy and healthy."

D4: I make myself feel frightened and helpless by demanding that Mom not use her age against me.

STEP 4: Construct one or more reprogramming statements from each demand statement.

R1: I can love and honor myself when Mom doesn't give me her approval.

Again, note the relationship between Jan's reprogramming statements and the demand

R2: I can be happy on the West Coast even without Mom's support.

R3: I can feel good about sending Mom a birthday present even when she doesn't write or call.

R4: I can love and care about myself when Mom uses her age against me on the telephone.

statements she fashioned in Step 3.

In this example Jan wound up using four reprogramming statements, and switching back from one to another as seemed appropriate. However, if working with several reprogramming statements simultaneously confuses you at first, work on one statement at a time, until you become more familiar with the reprogramming process.

STEP 5: **Focus intently on the upsetting images. Say or shout your demand statement(s) and intensify the negative feelings as much as possible. Continue until they peak. (Jan knelt in front of a large pillow and said she was ready to begin. We began by helping her focus on her negative images.)**

Q4: OK, now imagine your mother's face. She's sitting in the dining room by the telephone. It rings, and she answers. It's you. She begins talking, and then her face gets cold and sad . . . she looks so old . . . she sighs . . .

Q4: Helping Jan focus on the upsetting question.

A4: (Jan's eyes well up with tears) Yes, that's about how she looks . . .

Q5: Start!

A5: I upset myself by demanding that my mother not use her age against me!

Q6: Louder!

Q6: Make yourself experience and express your feelings as intensely as you possibly can. Pounding a pillow or using some other physical means of expression is optional, but we usually find that it helps.

A6: I make myself feel helpless by demanding that my mother not use her age! I make myself feel terrible by demanding . . . ! (Jan continues increasing the intensity of her demand statements for about 30 seconds. At one point she begins to sob, and is strongly reminded to continue upping the intensity even through her tears.)

STEP 6: **When the emotions peak, switch to your reprogramming statement. Continue as intensely as you can until the negative feelings begin to fade.**

Q7: OK, now switch!

A7: I can love and respect myself when Mom uses her age on the telephone!

Q8: Louder! Louder! Keep
the intensity up there!

A8: I *can care about myself even*   *A8:* Continue using your re-
when Mom uses her age on the   programming statement until
phone! I can . . . (Jan works for   you feel the emotions you've
about 45 seconds and then   been working on become sig-
lapses into panting silence.   nificantly less intense. Then
She still seems close to tears.   relax for a few seconds. This
That and a variety of other   doesn't mean you're finished.
non-verbal cues suggests to us   If, when you check your feel-
that she still has a cycle or six   ings level at Step 7 it turns out
to go.)   you're still upset, simply re-
                                turn to Step 5 and continue.

**STEP 7:   Relax. Check to see if you're still upset. If so,
return to Step 5. If the negative feelings are
substantially less or have disappeared, congratulations! Have a glass of water!**

Q9: How are you feeling?

A9: I don't know. I guess I feel   *A9:* Note that, while Jan isn't
really sad . . .   feeling much better, her ex-
                                perience of her negative feel-
                                ings has changed somewhat.
                                Before she was most in touch
                                with helplessness and frustra-
                                tion, now she reports feeling
                                sad. Complicated, long-stand-
                                ing issues such as parent-child
                                relationships often have sev-
                                eral negative emotions con-
                                nected with them. This is why
                                it sometimes helps to use more
                                than one reprogramming state-

ment. At any rate, Jan may find herself cycling through a variety of negative feelings before her reprogramming session is complete.

Q10: OK, good. Let's start again. I make myself feel . . .

A10: I make myself feel sad and lonely by demanding that Mom like the fact that I've moved. I make myself feel *lonely by demanding that* . . . (Jan cycles back through Steps 5-7 four times during these reprogramming exercises. Finally, on the fifth cycle, her emotional peak seems to break all at once. This is accompanied by a variety of vocal and non-verbal changes that generally signal that a trainee is close to success.)

A10: Now Jan will use reprogramming statement(s) connected with sadness and loss.

Jan's feelings of sadness soon turn to anger, first at her mother and then at herself. Then she begins to feel quite self-critical. Nevertheless, she keeps reprogramming, using whichever reprogramming statements seem to fit the particular feeling she is having at the moment.

A11: I can *care about myself* (almost a screech) even when Mom doesn't call me about the flowers (smiles) . . . I can care about myself even when (short laugh) *she doesn't call me* . . . (Jan lapses into silence, repeats her internal check, and then opens her eyes.)

A11: Humor, expressed in one form or another, is often a signal that a trainee has successfully reprogrammed a set of feelings (at least on one level) and has arrived at a good place to stop. Sometimes a trainee will find humor in the seriousness with which he's been taking his problem. The problem, the exercise, and everything connected with it will suddenly seem a little absurd. We consider this a very positive sign—but then the cosmic chuckle is always a good sign.

Q12: How do you feel?

A12: (smiling) Lighter . . . I don't know—it really changed that time . . . Right now I don't even CARE . . .

Q13: . . . that your mother didn't . . .

A13: . . . call me. That's one of her favorite ways of pouting. But you know, I just realized something! If you send a person a present NEEDING to get a response to feel good about it, it's not really a present, is it? I know my mother liked the flowers. But I think I sent them partly to try to get her on my side. And when it didn't work . . . (Shakes her head) . . .

A13: How true. We don't believe that insight or understanding of one's problems is a critical aspect of the behavior change process. Still, insight can prove valuable, and the "aha!" reaction can serve to reinforce the change that has just taken place. So we favor and support the insights of our trainees. However, in our work it is usually the behavior or emotional change that leads to the insight, rather than the other way around. At any rate, here Jan begins to show real willingness to accept responsibility for her part in the hostilities.

Q13: Maybe your mother sensed that too.

Q14: Gently prodding Jan to see her mother's side of the

story and possibly begin to let
her out of the doghouse.

A14: Yeah . . .

We don't mean to imply that either the reprogramming or the "insight" that Jan got during her workshop,
in and out of itself, will do much to strengthen her relationship with her mother or help her adjust to the West
Coast. The next time she and her mother have a difference
of opinion, she'll probably react pretty much the same way
she did this time. Jan is trying to carve out a life for herself
under conditions that are far from ideal, and doubtlessly
has some rocky times to look forward to. Nevertheless,
she's made a start. And if she practices her reprogramming skills regularly, and is willing to take responsibility
for her own negative feelings even when every ounce of her
being would rather make Mom the bad guy, gradually
things will begin to change.

In the final section of this chapter we will describe a
variation on the emotional reprogramming process designed for people who prefer to work silently and/or want
a reprogramming strategy that requires less physical exer-
tion.

The Tension-Release Method

As far as we know, the tension-release method of
emotional reprogramming was devised by Dr. Errol Shu-
bot of Saratoga, California, for those of his clients who
were unable or unwilling to pound pillows and scream.
Generally people with heart conditions, those who live

with others and don't have much privacy, those who have just had their tonsils out, or people who simply feel self-conscious when they yell and pound, might prefer the tension-release approach.

This procedure uses muscle tension and relaxation to assist in the reprogramming process. Although precisely how the technique works is unclear, one critical element seems to be the positive feeling which accompanies the change from exaggerated tension to deep relaxation. The procedure will work best for you if you already know how to relax your body reasonably well. If you don't, we suggest that you pick up a book or cassette tape on relaxation training and learn to do so. The value of the relaxation response goes way beyond its use in reprogramming exercises; an ability to relax is closely correlated to both physical and psychological well-being.

In this variation, complete Steps 1-4 in the manner described above. Then proceed as follows:

STEP 5: Focus on the images and fantasies that are causing you to be upset. Exaggerate their impact, letting yourself become as upset as possible. Simultaneously, tense every muscle in your body as tightly as you can. Begin repeating your demand statement, either silently or aloud, but with as much intensity and force as possible. Continue until your negative feelings peak.

Again, your job is to duplicate and intensify the negative feelings you wish to reprogram. Exaggerate these feelings as much as possible. As you do so be aware of the discomfort and the other feelings produced by your exaggerated tension level.*

There's no need to shout in this exercise, and you can say your demand statements silently if you wish. However, saying them out loud may help you focus on them more clearly. Whichever method you choose, repeat them over and over again, and say them as if you mean them.

STEP 6: **When your negative feelings have peaked and your tension level is as high as you're able or willing to make it, switch to your reprogramming sentence(s). Keeping your body tense, say your reprogramming sentence *once*, as intensely as you can. *Then* take a deep breath, and let it out in a rush. As you exhale, allow your body to relax completely. Relax your body all at once, not gradually. Continue to focus on the upsetting images and repeat your reprogramming statement. With each repetition see if you can get your body to relax more and more. If at this point you find yourself getting more upset, immediately return to Step 4 and proceed.**

Note the order of change described above. First, tense your body and say your demand statement. When your upset peaks and your body is as tense as it can get, say your reprogramming statement once. Only then do you allow your body to relax. The idea is that, among other things,

---

*Physical tension is important in this exercise, but we do suggest that you exercise a little reason. Some of the muscles in your body are very strong. Don't tense so hard that your thigh muscles cramp or you put a crack in your new $900 bridgework.

the change from demand to reprogramming statement is rewarded by the positive feelings of relaxation.

You may feel yourself become upset almost as soon as you begin to relax. If the negative feelings seem less intense than they were before, continue to repeat your reprogramming statement and relax more deeply. Perhaps they will begin to fade. If, as you continue to focus on the upsetting images the negative feeling also continues to get worse, then return to Step 4. The problem is that relaxation is a passive response (literally the absence of tension) whereas emotional expression is a very active response. Therefore, many people find it hard to attain or maintain a state of relaxation when upset, while the same level of upset would probably increase their ability to scream. Consequently, trainees who use this reprogramming method often find themselves cycling through Steps 5 and 6 more often than trainees using the emotive method.

We suggest you spend a minimum of five or ten seconds attempting to relax after switching to your reprogramming statement. If you feel less upset, continue with Step 5 for 20 to 30 seconds longer before moving on.

STEP 7: **Stop repeating your reprogramming sentence(s) and allow your mind to be relaxed and calm for a few seconds. Then check your work. Deliberately think of the upsetting experience and notice if you still feel as upset as you did before you began. If you do, return to Step 4. If you feel substantially less upset you may stop or continue working, as you wish.**

In the tension-release method, Steps 5 and 6 tend to

flow together. Most people automatically check their emotions when they begin relaxing in Step 5. Still, it's important to do so again after you stop directing your energies into your reprogramming statement.

Again, the tension-release method usually take more repetitions than the emotive variation does. It's not uncommon for a trainee to cycle back and forth between tension and release 15 to 30 times before noticing a significant drop in his negative feelings.

Remember to look for changes in emotional quality as well as intensity. That is, sadness may change to anger, anger to helplessness, helplessness to guilt, etc. It's important to pay close attention and reprogram the emotion you're feeling now, not the one you were feeling five minutes ago.

Most of the other suggestions offered for the emotive variation of emotional reprogramming apply to the release method as well. In particular remember this: DON'T STOP IN THE MIDDLE. Continue to work until the intensity of your negative feelings begins to come down.

In general, we have found the tension-release variation of emotional reprogramming to be less powerful than the emotive variation. Nonetheless, it is a valuable technique; there are a great many people who simply will not or can not use the more intense variation. In addition, we found individuals who responded beautifully to the tension-release method after having tried the emotive method without success. We say again, people are different. It is most important to experiment with a variety of reprogramming techniques, in order to find the ones that work best for you.

Streamlining

At first, emotional reprogramming may seem like a complicated, tedious, and rather time-consuming process. There are several steps to remember, certain specific sentence forms to be used, etc. In the beginning you will probably find that the process of using emotional reprogramming is indeed rather involved. Fortunately, however, that will not always be the case.

Remember what it was like when you learned to drive a car? It seemed like there were 55 things to remember to do just to get the darn thing moving. Climb in, fasten the seat belt, adjust the mirror, adjust the other mirror, put the car in neutral, put the keys in the ignition, turn on the ignition, release the brake, put the car in gear, etc., etc. But now, years later, it doesn't seem so tedious anymore. It seems as though you simply jump in the car, do a few things, and drive away. Your biocomputer does most of the preparation and driving for you, automatically. You no longer go through the various unnecessary movements, confusions, time-consuming errors, and other miscellaneous patterns that you used while you were learning to drive. Driving a car is still as complicated as it ever was, but you've streamlined your driving strategies until they have become very efficient for you.

If you're willing to practice "by the numbers" in the beginning, eventually your reprogramming strategies will streamline in the same fashion. For one thing, you'll begin to think automatically in terms of demand statements, reprogramming statements, and so on. You won't have to stop to figure out whether or not you are using the right format, or have chosen the right issue to work on. Second, you'll learn which parts of the procedures work for you, and which parts you don't need. Hanging on to the former and dropping the latter will speed things up a lot. Third, you'll begin to get a better idea as to when it's best for you to move from one step to another, when you need a new reprogramming statement, when it's time to stop, and other issues that can be confusing in the beginning.

More important still, the reprogramming option will begin to occur to you automatically in the face of stress. After taking our workshops, most trainees report that they go through several mental steps before they even think of reprogramming:

"Oh, God! The boss gave me a dirty look. And he didn't even say hello to me! Maybe I'd better resign and get it over with. I'd rather starve than go through this again!"

"Oh-oh, there I go again, leaping to conclusions and getting all upset. What other options do I have?"

"I could go in and tell him I don't like it when he doesn't say hello to me. But I'd probably start crying. Also, I think he's got meetings all morning."

"It's almost time for my coffee break. Gee, I might be able to use emotional reprogramming!"

"Now how do you do that again?"

But if you practice, awareness of the reprogramming option and of how to apply it efficiently will soon come to you automatically when you feel upset. When some idiot cuts you off on the freeway and you're about to put your foot through the floor to catch him and teach him a lesson he'll never forget, you'll automatically say to yourself, "No, wait. . . ." Then you'll pull off the freeway for a few minutes, start pounding the car seat, and yelling, "I can feel like a man (or woman) even when I let somebody cut me off. . . ."

If you use it enough, the procedure may streamline further still. Eventually you may find the entire emotional reprogramming process occurring spontaneously in the face of a potential upset, and in a manner that short-circuits your negative feelings almost before they have a chance to begin. Your boss stomps by your desk and into his office without saying good morning. But that little voice in your head doesn't immediately start criticizing you or drumming up worst-possibles. Instead it croons, "Well, I can care about myself even when the boss gives me a dirty look. I can relax and have a good day even when he doesn't say hello to me." Your body relaxes a little. You smile for a moment, capturing just a bit of the cosmic chuckle as you think of how silly you'd been, reacting so strongly to your boss's moods. Suddenly you realize you've just reprogrammed yourself "on the hoof" quickly enough to prevent a negative reaction from occurring in the first place.

To repeat, if emotional reprogramming seems a tedious, time-consuming process, that's as it should be. While you're learning it, it is a tedious and time-consuming process, just like learning to drive a car once was. As you keep practicing, your reprogramming strategies will begin to streamline, become more automatic and efficient. Eventually you'll be able to deal with major upsets much more quickly and effectively than you can now, and minor upsets will seem to almost reprogram themselves.

SUMMARY

Emotional reprogramming is a procedure that combines the sequencing tactics we're presented in Chapter 5 with the duplication tactics discussed in Chapter 6. It works by training you to respond to potentially upsetting situations with positive self-statements rather than with self-criticism or other negative material. Emotional reprogramming is a good technique to use when you are already upset. As a matter of fact, we tell our trainees that upsets actually provide a grand opportunity to practice reprogramming! Learning to reframe problems as opportunities in this manner will help you avoid that most deadly form of emotional circularity: getting upset about being upset.

The emotive form of emotional reprogramming described in this chapter is not for everyone. If you feel uncomfortable at the idea of pounding and yelling loudly, or if the circumstances of your life argue against exerting yourself or making a lot of noise, then use the tension-release programming method described later in the chapter. We have found both variations to work quite well.

Nevertheless, we believe that there is nothing intrinsically dangerous about the emotive procedure described here. We've used it with a wide variety of people and problems without complication. There's really only one important rule to remember. As with any duplication technique, once begun it must be continued until the intensity of the target emotion has begun to lessen. If you consciously intensify a negative emotion and then leave yourself at the heightened level or try to cover up the feeling in some fashion, you may sensitize rather than desensitize yourself to the situation you've been working with. So once you start, keep going until your mood begins to lighten, until you begin feeling less upset. NEVER STOP IN THE MIDDLE.

8

Reprogramming
Irrational Beliefs

Throughout this book we've been giving you examples of how people's beliefs and assumptions can keep them from reaching their goals. Mary would like to meet a man, but because she believes she'll never have a successful experience with one, she shuns the parties and social clubs where men hang out. Joanne believes that if her husband Andy loved her, he wouldn't come home late from the office. Her reaction when he does show up ruins her evening and his. Jan's belief that she needs her mother's support to make it in her new life on the West Coast serves only to make her feel miserable. For that matter, the belief that the earth was flat kept explorers out of the New World for hundreds of years.

We don't mean to imply that we see anything wrong with beliefs and assumptions *per se*. On the contrary, belief systems can be valuable and adaptive mechanisms which provide order and predictability in a confusing, often hostile world. For instance, religious convictions give many people the support and initiative to deal effectively with crisis situations which otherwise might be overwhelming. When we "believe in ourselves," we're generally much more able to deal with the situation at hand than otherwise, and our chances of coming out ahead are usually better as well.

Belief systems don't even have to be valid to be valuable. A man once survived a boating accident by swimming several miles to shore. Later, he told reporters that he considered himself a mediocre swimmer. He said he thought he'd capsized much closer to shore, and had he known how far he needed to swim, he probably would have given up.

The trick, of course, is to adopt beliefs and assumptions that work for you. Belief systems impose arbitrary rules and standards on people. When these rules and standards begin to lead us elsewhere than toward the goals we set, it's time to consider reprogramming the underlying beliefs.

FALLACY PATTERNS

Consider the eleven common irrational beliefs listed in the box on the next page. Translated to the printed page and presented in black and white, most of these beliefs do indeed seem irrational. So it's surprising how many of them crop up anyway. Dr. Albert Ellis, who created the list, believes that literally millions of people indulge in this kind of thinking—with devastating results. Read the list

ELEVEN COMMON IRRATIONAL BELIEFS*

1) The idea that it is a dire necessity for an adult human being to be loved or approved of by virtually every significant other person in his community.

2) The idea that one should be thoroughly competent, adequate, and achieving in all possible respects if one is to consider oneself worthwhile.

3) The idea that certain people are bad, wicked, or villainous and that they should be punished for their villainy.

4) The idea that it is awful and catastrophic when things are not the way one would very much like them to be.

5) The idea that human unhappiness is externally caused and that people have little or no ability to control their sorrows and disturbances.

6) The idea that if something is or may be dangerous or fearsome one should be terribly concerned about it and should keep dwelling on the possibility of its occurring.

7) The idea that it is easier to avoid than to face certain life difficulties and self-responsibilities.

8) The idea that one should be dependent on others and need someone stronger than oneself on whom to rely.

9) The idea that one's past history is an all-important determinant of one's present behavior and that because something once strongly affected one's life, it should indefinitely have similar effects.

10) The idea that one should become quite upset over other people's problems and disturbances.

11) The idea that there is invariably a right, precise and perfect solution to human problems and that it is catastrophic if this correct solution is not found.

*This list was compiled by Dr. Albert Ellis, founder of the school of Rational-Emotive Therapy (RET). His list of rational beliefs is presented and discussed in detail in *Reason and Emotion in Psychotherapy*, New York: Lyle Stewart, 1962.

again. How many of these "irrational beliefs" do you think may, at one time or another, have influenced you?

Dr. Ellis' list of irrational beliefs has been discussed, analyzed, copied, and reanalyzed a great deal since its publication in 1962. So in this chapter, we'd like to take a different tack. Dr. Ellis presents his list on what may be called "a content level." That is, the list contains sentences that people might actually say to themselves in order to maintain a belief. In the following pages we intend to discuss belief systems from a "structural" level instead. Perhaps "strategic" might be a better word for it. At any rate, we'd like to discuss certain patterns of thought and strategy that provide a framework for a great variety of specific irrational beliefs. We call these patterns *fallacies*.

Fallacy patterns grow out of the inability of our bio-computers to accurately store information they take in from the real world, and a further inability to process that information accurately and thoroughly once it's stored. As far as we're concerned, human beings do not have the sensory apparatus to experience the world as it really is, nor do they have the psychological apparatus to process their memories of that experience. To paraphrase Roy Blount, we're all about three bricks shy of a load as far as our ability to deal with sensory and psychological data is concerned.

If that seems to be something of an overstatement, consider the chair you're sitting in as you read this book. Physicists tell us that it is composed mostly of empty space. Does it seem like empty space to you? We'll bet it feels pretty solid. Similarly, Einstein's theory of relativity seems outlandishly paradoxical for any kind of a "common sense" model. Yet research physicists not only tell us he was right, but are coming up with data that are beginning to make Einstein's concepts seem almost provincial.*

We experience the world around us in a manner that reflects the limitations of our sensory apparatus, rather than the way the world "really is." Then we act on and respond to our maps, or representations, of the world—not on or to the world itself. In general, we tend to get in trouble when our maps are wildly inaccurate representations of the world as it really is. So if that tree outside your window looks sturdy to you, and you feel the inclination to climb it, you may be in for a nasty fall if an unseen flaw in the trunk gives way when you are 15 or 20 feet off the ground.

Actually, it's hard to get into serious trouble with a tree: possibly a few broken bones here and there. But when we try to map and process such experiences as "love," or "God," things get very complicated very quickly. Deletions, distortions, subjective interpretations, and other inaccuracies abound. And out of this morass of subjectivity grow arbitrary beliefs that can blindly influence our experiences of "reality," our loved ones, and ourselves.

Reframing Fallacy Patterns

To reframe an experience literally means to change the structure of your viewpoint of that experience. George's doctor tells him he has an ulcer. George imme-

*For a fascinating description of the similarities between psychology and particle physics, see Zukov, G. *The Dancing Wu-Li Masters.* New York: Morrow Quill Paperbacks, 1978.

diately thinks of the three six-packs of beer he won't be able to drink while watching the football games every Saturday, and becomes upset. Of course his anger and disappointment really have little to do with the ulcer or with the beer he isn't going to be able to drink. The negative feelings stem from the perspective, or viewpoint, that George is taking about his ulcer, and from the negative anticipations which naturally follow. George defines his ulcer as a problem which is going to keep him from having certain enjoyable experiences over the next few weeks.

If he is not going to spend valuable time mourning lost six packs and snapping at his wife, George is going to have to reframe the experience of his stomach problem. Imagine what would happen, for instance, if George looked upon the ulcer as an opportunity to maintain a strict diet that would help him take off fifteen pounds he would honestly like to lose. From that viewpoint, his anticipations would be positive; he still wouldn't particularly like having an ulcer, but the reality of the ulcer would be a lot less noxious for him—and probably would put a lot less pressure on his marriage as well.

We don't mean to sound Pollyannaish about this. We don't believe that positive thinking alone will ever cure the ills of humanity and bring lasting peace and happiness to all. Life has its ups and downs. But George can't do anything about having an ulcer. Making himself and his family miserable about it for a month or so isn't going to help and may make matters worse. Given the realities of his situation, he may as well reframe his problem as an opportunity to lose some weight, rather than develop a second ulcer worrying about the first one.

Neither do we mean to imply that reframing is an easy thing to do. A part of George is really going to miss those six packs, and he may have to work hard to develop the more positive perspective. We believe that it will be energy well spent.

Reframing is the one reprogramming strategy we discuss in this book that does not involve formal goal specification and barrier analysis. However, it does help to be able to pinpoint fallacy patterns imbedded in the structure of the viewpoint to be reframed. For instance, George needs to recognize that he's turning his ulcer into a problem and would be better off making it into an opportunity or a project instead.

Essentially, reprogramming belief systems is a three-step process. First, *recognize* the logical fallacy imbedded in your negative belief. Describe it in as much detail as you can. Look for related assumptions, beliefs, and irrational thought patterns that may be supporting it.

Second, *replace* the fallacy pattern with a more productive, positive one. Some of the ways this can be done will be discussed below. Sometimes simply recognizing the fallacy will be enough to begin reprogramming it. In other cases, hours of work will be required. Usually, the negative belief will support and be supported by a variety of more specific barrier systems and sequences as well. When this is the case, reframing can be combined with other reprogramming strategies described in this book. Emotional reprogramming, as described in Chapter 7, is often of particular value.

Third, *practice* the new viewpoint pattern until you begin to use it automatically. Again, there are a variety of ways to do this. However, often simply remembering to use it is most important (and most difficult) at this stage.

Sometimes you'll find it easy to maintain your new perspective once you have successfully reframed it. Usually, however, changing a perspective requires a lot of practice. Belief systems involve complicated sequences of emotional and behavioral habits, and the habit patterns involved usually take quite a while to change. As we've mentioned time and again in this book, there is no substitute for diligent, repetitive practice.

In the course of helping people reprogram, we have isolated certain fallacy patterns that come up over and over again in the belief systems of our trainees. Remember, fallacy patterns are imbedded in the structure underlying the belief system; the content of the belief system varies from trainee to trainee and from situation to situation. In the course of this chapter we will discuss eight of the most common fallacy patterns. In each case we will first describe the pattern itself, and then give a couple of examples showing how it arises and how it can be reframed.

The Either-Or Fallacy

We've run into the Either-Or Fallacy several times in previous chapters. This is a mental set in which an individual automatically assumes that there are only two ways a situation can be resolved, limiting himself to two ways of responding to a particular situation at hand. In other words, he anticipates winning or losing, either having to give in to an attack or fight back against it, being either accepted or rejected by a potential date, and so on.

The fallacy, of course, is that most real-life situations are not dichotomous. Usually, more than two outcomes are possible and there are usually several ways of responding to a particular situation. Nevertheless, many times people fall into what S. I. Hayakawa* called the "two-valued orientation." And the results can be devastating. This is the most common, and one of the most deadly, of the fallacy patterns. We believe that a great deal of human conflict and suffering can be traced back to one variation or another of the Either-Or fallacy. As a matter of fact, most of the fallacy patterns described in this chapter will have an either-or component imbedded in them someplace. Because this pattern is so prevalent, we'd like to distinguish between two sub-categories of the Either-Or fallacy, and then spend a little time with each.

Giving in vs. Fighting Back

Human beings seem to be particularly prone to dichotomous reasoning when they feel stressed or under attack. It's difficult for many people to think of anything to do other than give in to the attack (by either giving up or running away) or fight back against it. Yet there is almost always a third alternative available.

Recall Jan (Chapter 7), who was angry and hurt because her mother hadn't acknowledged a birthday gift. She wanted to phone and straighten things out, but was afraid to make the call.

It was dichotomous reasoning that kept Jan away from the telephone. She anticipated that her mother would criticize her or try to make her feel guilty for moving to the West Coast. In her distress, Jan believed she

*An interesting discussion of dichotomous reasoning may be found in Hayakawa, S. I., *Language in Thought and Action.* New York: Harcourt, Brace, and World, 1964.

had only two ways of dealing with her mother's position: giving in to it by crying, admitting she was lonely in San Francisco and had been wrong to move, admitting to the guilt she felt, etc.), or struggling against it (by arguing with her mother, becoming angry and aggressive on the phone, or various other things she knew she'd feel horrible about as soon as she hung up). The truth is that Jan had a third alternative she couldn't see—in fact it took a considerable amount of emotional reprogramming before she was able to see it. But the third alternative was there, nonetheless.

At this point let us digress for a moment. We talked about the concept of the "third alternative" briefly in Chapter 2 when we discussed the philosophy of assertive yielding. Yielding can indeed be a goal-directed strategy, and often provides a marvelous alternative to giving in or fighting back.

Many third alternative strategies are modeled after Eastern martial arts tactics used in such practices as Judo and Aikido. Rather than giving in to or fighting against an antagonist, the Aikido master attempts to blend with the antagonist's movement and energy. If successful, he matches or duplicates it so precisely that he begins to be able to control it. The Aikido master would tell us that an attacker is, by definition, off-center; and that it is the job of the Aikido player to help his adversary regain a centered, tranquil position. If the adversary is, say, attacking with a knife, this might involve helping him to drop his knife, or to lie down:

"First you must *join* with your attacker. Get along side him or her. Agree with his right to feel whatever it is he's feeling. You're not necessarily agreeing with him about everything, but it certainly won't cost you anything to empathize. Become confluent. After all, he may be in the wrong, but you can't argue with the obvious fact that he is upset. Everyone is entitled to feel.

"What most often (happens next) is the pause. This occurs when the attacker is trying to make sense out of what's just happened. (The defender) can then begin to lead . . . In the physical realm of martial arts, there is always that brief moment when, because of the defender's response, the attacker loses his balance. At that precise moment, the defender is in charge and must take care of the attacker, helping him to a new, firmer, less-aggressive balance. In our experience in the non-physical realm, that loss of balance is usually heralded by a pause. You must learn to listen carefully for that pause. When it comes, take care of your attacker. Lead him to harmony."*

Thus, the martial arts form gives us a valuable alternative to giving in or fighting back. The first step, of course, is to be aware while under attack that we do have a third alternative available. That's where reframing comes in. (Sometimes this particular reframe takes a while to learn.) If the reframe is successful, giving in and fighting back—the issue of winning or losing, in general—become irrelevant. Obviously, it's one thing to display "make

*From *Giving In To Get Your Way*, by Terry Dobson and Victor Miller (pp. 99-103). (Dobson is a San Francisco psychologist who spent several years in the Orient studying Aikido. He now trains people to use Aikido philosophies and skills on verbal as well as non-verbal battlegrounds.)

love, not war" posters in one's bedroom and another to deal noncombatively with an enraged attacker intent on beating one to a physical or psychological pulp. Still, Aikido trainees are taught to meet physical attack with exactly that attitude.

Precisely the same principles apply when the attack is psychological rather than physical—where the weapons are words or implications, and points are scored in terms of frustrations, hurt feelings, and guilt. Paradoxically, when the defender stops defending and begins to blend and harmonize with the attack, his/her position often immediately becomes much stronger and his/her probability of winning much greater should the interaction remain on a competitive level.

Strategically, applying a third alternative point of view involves three independent steps. Each of these should be visualized at length during reprogramming. First, you must be absolutely clear that the situation is not one of attack-defend or win-lose, but rather one calling for sensitivity, empathy and aid. You must practice until you can maintain this point of view while under attack, as well as while in the comparative safety of workshops and reprogramming sessions. Second, pay careful attention to the precise manner and style of the attack so you can effectively blend and harmonize with the energies involved. This may mean, among other things, listening carefully to those hateful words and closely observing those holier-than-thou facial expressions your antagonist is using for emphasis. Third, and most important, your job is to give your opponent what he or she needs in order to drop the attacking posture—in a manner that leaves both of you unharmed and in a position to gain something from the interaction if possible.

Tactically, there is a wide variety of techniques that can be used to implement third alternatives. Many involve the use of good communication tools, such as non-critical acknowledgement, active listening, and the use of "I statements." Sometimes the situation calls for a bit of on-the-spot creativity. The hard part, however, isn't getting to know third alternative tactics. There really is no set of "third alternative tactics" beyond the reframe itself. The hard part is remembering, under stress, not to fall back into the old give-in fight-back pattern.*

Now back to Jan. Once emotional reprogramming has taken some of the edge off her anger and guilt, it will be time for her to reframe the adversarial position she has taken with her mother. When Jan realizes that she no longer has to choose between fighting her mother's barbs and getting stabbed by them, she'll be free of a conflict that's plagued her in one way or another for years.

Negative Anticipations

We live in a competitive world—one in which issues of winning and losing, success and failure, acceptance and rejection, really do come up. Still, during our three score and ten on this planet most of us will have many opportunities for success, popularity and happiness. The chance to play wide receiver in the Super Bowl or run for president of the senior class may only come around once—but these are exceptions rather than the rule. Most win-lose

---

*Although it's relatively easy to discuss the third alternative philosophy, learning to employ it well under high-stress conditions takes practice. Space limits us from describing in this book the training tactics we use. They are detailed in Piaget, G. W., and Binkley, B. J., *How To Communicate Under Pressure: Dealing Effectively With Difficult People*. Portola Vallye: IAHB Press, 1983.

situations are repetitive ones. Single young men generally hope to approach attractive strangers many times in their lives; most real estate salespeople assume they will have the opportunity to sell a lot of houses, and so on.

But some people, caught between the horns of an either-or pattern miss the very positive implications of this guaranteed repetition. Rather than see the role of "single man" or "computer salesperson" as a long-term commitment to a process that will certainly include many successes and many failures, one which therefore should be judged in the long run on a percentage basis, we instead view our encounters as a series of independent trials— each with a final, all-or-nothing outcome attached to it. As a consequence, we must deal with the worst of both worlds: the endless repetition of long-term involvement with none of the built-in security such involvement usually provides, and the terrifying do-or-die intensity of a one shot deal, but with no relief in sight.

Imagine that you're a real estate saleswoman. You've decided to farm a new territory for residential listings. ("Farming a territory" means picking a neighborhood, and then knocking on doors or phoning, introducing yourself to everyone in the area, handing out cards, and mainly hoping that someone has been thinking or will be thinking of selling his/her house.) Ninety-nine out of every hundred people you contact will not be interested in selling, and a few of them will get nasty while telling you so. If you're at all sensitive to rejection, you're in for a hard time. "Farming" is a fine way to build a real estate practice; but after ten or twenty negative responses, a great many people who try it begin thinking seriously of going back to teaching high school math.

The culprit, once again, is dichotomous reasoning. When you're dealing with repetitive rather than individual occurences, the trick is to amortize your wins over your losses. In philosophy, this point of view is called "and-both" (as opposed to "either-or").

A real estate woman in one of our workshops told us she'd had it: she was going to hang up her rake and overalls for good. We counseled her as follows. (Note the "amortization" reframe we used.)

"From what you've told us, you think that on the average you'd have to contact 50 or 75 families in order to get a good shot at a real estate listing. Let's be conservative, and call it 100 contacts for a single listing. Now, you've also said the average home in your area sells for about $100,000. Figuring your half of the commission at 3%, that makes each initial contact worth, on the average, $30. Now listen carefully. When you knock on a door and get it slammed in your face, we want you to respond as follows: step back, bow politely, and say, "Thank you for the $30" to the closed door. Then move on to the next house, and earn $30 more."

The same tactic works at singles clubs, when starting conversations at cocktail parties, and while playing roulette at Lake Tahoe. (Of course, it works in reverse at Lake Tahoe.) We repeat: this is not a trick. The reasoning is valid. Individual situations *are* trivial in sales work and singles bars. No matter what the situation, you will almost always get another chance. And with 100 or 1000 chances ahead of you, you are virtually assured of getting some "wins." Under repetitive circumstances think and work from an "and-both," not an "either-or" model. The long-term probabilities are what count.

The If-Then Fallacy

These are also variously known as *implied cause* or *false cause* patterns. Actually, if-then patterns and either-or patterns are variations on the same theme. For example, the if-then statement, "If you really loved me, then you'd take off your clothes," translates easily into the either-or form: "Either I will get you to undress, or I will think that you don't love me."

If-then statements are often used to convey indirect, coercive, or manipulative messages. The statement, "If you give a damn about this company, you'd be willing to work late tonight," is intended to make the receiver either agree to put in some overtime and/or feel guilty for preferring to leave. If-then statements imply a causal connection between the two issues mentioned (in this case caring about the company and putting in overtime)—issues which may well be completely independent of one another. In our workshops we train people to recognize this pattern. Then they learn to separate the issues and illuminate the implied causal connection between them. This forces the sender either to take responsibility for his implication, or to take the implication back. In the illustration above, the employee might respond, "So because I've decided not to stay late tonight, you think I don't care about our company very much?" Even if the sender responds in the affirmative, his assertion is now expressed rather than implied and can be dealt with more directly.

Learning to deal with if-then communications has considerable value. But, as with either-or patterns, the most important and most deadly consequence of the if-then fallacy occurs when the pattern becomes imbedded in our own thinking. In Chapter 3 we mentioned Randy, who, on the way home from work, says to himself, "If my wife loves me, she'll have dinner ready when I get home." He arrives home, finds that dinner isn't ready, and begins to feel unloved. In the "real world" there is no necessary connection between dinner preparation and spousal love. Nevertheless, if Randy repeats, "If she loves me, she'll have dinner ready" to himself enough times, he can literally program himself to feel uncared for when he sees an empty supper table. Neither does this process have to be conscious; Randy may not recognize that he's trapped in an if-then pattern at all. He may simply drive home with his conscious mind on idle, go inside, and begin to feel lonely without knowing why.

Reframing the if-then perspective involves, first of all, recognizing that it exists. This is not always easy to do. Whether the implications originate from someone else or from within your own head, they can be extremely subtle. Further, if-then implications can be couched in a variety of semantic forms, including the either-or form.

Once you recognize an if-then pattern, restate it in a way that illuminates and specifies the causal implication involved. Then consider it carefully. Is there any chance that the two issues are not causally related? If there is any chance that they are independent of each other, restate the sentence in a way that illuminates their separateness. At least for reprogramming purposes, never assume or imply a cause-effect relationship between issues that have the slightest chance of being independent. A great many philosophers and psychologists, including Carl Jung, believe that the Western idea of causality (that some things cause other things to occur) is in its entirety no more than a reflection of the way we've learned to think and speak.★

We don't mean to suggest that you give up your beliefs about cause and effect. Even the most "Eastern" of thinkers act as if causality exists when confronted by a large angry dog, or when they find a costly error in a bank statement. But some people are very quick to assign a causal connection where none exists or where the situation is ambiguous—thereby creating problems for themselves.

So pause for a moment the next time your wife surprises you while you're painting the garage, and you knock three quarts of canary-yellow oil-base paint onto your new Irish Setter. Sneering in chauvinist glee and snarling "Damn it, honey, see what you made me do!?" may not be quite as righteous and accurate as you once thought it was.

The Golden Rule Fallacy

The Golden Rule reads, "Do unto others as you would have others do unto you." Ideally, the Golden Rule seems like a fine goal toward which to strive. It's humanitarian; it sounds fair; if everyone abided by it, we have no doubt that the world would be a better place in which to live.

But pragmatically, the Golden Rule just doesn't work very well. Human beings differ from one another in terms of their priorities, needs, tastes, and patterns of communication; they function best when dealt with in terms of their individual needs, priorities, and preferences. We believe that the Golden Rule should actually read, "Do unto others

★See Jung's, "Introduction" to the *I Ching, The Chinese Book of Changes.*

as others would have you do unto them." But it doesn't, so the Golden Rule Fallacy occurs with regularity.

The actual fallacy here is imbedded in an assumption universal among small children: "Everyone is like me!" As we mature, some of us learn that people are different and thus have different preferences. But we still find it hard to act that way. "Everyone is like me" is imbedded so deeply in our nature that the Golden Rule can be over-ridden only with considerable effort.

Consider two friends of ours we'll call Joan and Gerry. Over the years, both have evolved effective ways to relax after a hard day's work. Unfortunately, these methods differ markedly from one another. When Gerry comes home in the evening, he likes to get away by himself for awhile. He'll sit in his study, stare out the window at his favorite tree, maybe have a beer, and in one way or another spend a half an hour or so by himself. Soon, he no longer feels pressured or stressed by thoughts of work; and is ready to spend an evening of shared intimacy with his wife. However, if he doesn't get that half hour—say, Joan comes and throws her arms around him when he walks in the door and begins to recount her day—he feels smothered by what he considers to be inconsiderate demands.

On the other hand, Joan wants some attention during those first few minutes after she gets home. She's ministered to others for several hours, and now she wants to be touched, cuddled, talked to, and generally nurtured herself. This helps her recharge her emotional batteries, which have been drained somewhat by the demands of her daily routine. If Gerry were to treat her the way he would wish to be treated in her place, she would feel ignored, unappreciated, and possibly unloved.

Yet most people do exactly that! It's natural, when we're trying to be nice to one another, to follow the old Golden Rule. And for people like Joan and Gerry it doesn't work at all. Gerry feels smothered, Joan feels ignored, neither understands what the hell is going on, and both are only trying to be nice!

A variation on the Golden Rule Fallacy occurs commonly (and ironically) in the psychotherapist's office. Most therapists tend to teach their patients and clients the particular "language of psychotherapy" that happens to accompany their particular conceptual biases. Psychodynamic therapists soon have their clients talking about repressed drives, superegos, and libidinal cathexis; transactional analysists speak of lifescripts, critical parents, and game analysis; and so on. Critics of the psychotherapy movement have gone so far as to suggest that the primary goal of treatment is the learning of therapeutic jargon. The client leaves the therapy sessions essentially unhelped. But he has learned to frame his problems in a new language system, and for that reason feels temporarily less troubled by them. When the discomfort returns, he'll simply find another therapist and learn another language.

Frankly, we don't think it's quite that bad. However, we would agree with Milton Erickson's contention that therapy works best when the clinician learns the client's language and personal idiosyncracies, rather than the other way around.

Reframe the Golden Rule. People are different: do unto others as others would have you do unto them, and you'll go further for it. Learning the other person's language, of course, is a skill that is basic to all forms of effective communication. Crack salespeople do it naturally. Effective communicators in all walks of life pay careful attention to those with whom they wish to communicate, and then employ the words, body posturing, references, metaphors, and other communication vehicles which the other person will be able to receive and process most easily.

Step 1 in learning to reframe the Golden Rule is: *pay attention!* That may sound simplistic, however most of us don't pay much attention at all to the person we're talking to. We're too busy trying to figure out what we're going to say next.

Once we learn what the other person's styles and preferences are, Step 2 involves learning to duplicate them ourselves. For instance, if George wants to sell a Porsche to a very feeling-oriented individual, he needs to learn to talk in terms of the feel of the car as it corners, the tightness of the suspension, and the grip of the tires on the road. However, if his customer is a visual thinker George might instead describe the metallic sheen of the red paint and the clear view of the countryside afforded by the sun roof.

We're happy to report that Gerry and Joan eventually learned to "speak one another's language." Now when Joan comes home, Gerry puts his arms around her, holds her tight, and says, "Hi, lover. How was your day?" Gerry feels a little like he's smothering her—but Joan loves it. On the other hand, when Gerry walks in the door, Joan throws him a beer, sings out, "Hi, honey!" and leaves him alone for a half an hour. She feels as if she's acting a little cold, but she knows it works. At last report they were doing famously.*

The Generalization Fallacy

Generalization, as far as we know, is a learning strategy common to all organisms on earth and absolutely necessary for survival. The gazelle learns to run from female lions as well as from male lions; our dog Bozo need be sprayed by only one or two skunks before he acquires a very clear understanding of certain characteristics inherent to all skunks. However, as animals mature, they must learn to differentiate as well as generalize; that is, they must learn to recognize the differences as well as the similarities among things. When an irrational prejudice or belief short-circuits the process of differentiation, what we call the generalization fallacy occurs. Curiously, the generalization fallacy appears to be particularly widespread throughout the species known as man.

The person who overgeneralizes sees all psychiatrists as phony, all women as emotional, and all Dobermans as vicious. On the positive side, he might see all nurses as veritable angels of mercy, despite repeated evidence to the contrary. He may go to Mexico on vacation, be treated nicely by a bellhop on arrival, and come home two weeks later thoroughly pleased with the miserable service and rotten food he "enjoyed" for the balance of his stay.

---

*From time to time a trainee will ask, "What happens when Joan and Gerry come home together? Who gets his/her needs met?" Or, "What happens when Gerry doesn't *want* to meet Joan's needs?" These questions give us the chance to mention that there is room for compromise in any relationship and that *no* reframing strategy will ever take the place of a willingness to give. If and when you *are* willing to give, though, the Golden Rule reframe may help you give more skillfully.

Generalizers, of course, tend to be prejudiced as well, and to operate from very rigid and highly-defined value systems. In its worst form, this is a tremendously difficult fallacy pattern to overcome.

Use specification procedures to reprogram a tendency to generalize. Apply the questioning strategies demonstrated in Chapters 2 and 4. Set specific reprogramming goals: that is, pick specific generalizations on which you would like to focus. First, break the generalization down into see/hear/feel terms. Then see if you can find specific exceptions to it. Ultimately you will have reframed your generalization in relative rather than absolute terms. (For instance, the position, "All psychiatrists are phony" may eventually be replaced by the position, "Some psychiatrists are phony, and some aren't," or "Most psychiatrists are phony." Even the declaration, "All psychiatrists are phony except for Jerry and Alan" may be a start.

As always, the first step in reframing generalization fallacies lies in recognizing the fact that your perspective is being limited by them. If you know that you are a generalizer and would like to work on it, we congratulate you. You're not as badly off as some folks we've run into, and are already part way home.

The Nominalization Fallacy

When you nominalize something you give it a label. When Peter says, "I'm a married man," the label "married" summarizes a wealth of information about Peter's home life, (apparent) availability, and socio-cultural status. Pointing to the glowing monster across the room and saying, "That is a television set," communicates more in one sentence than five minutes of detailed description possibly could. The process of labeling, or nominalizing, things is inextricably embedded in the development of language. For all practical purposes, normal human beings over the age of three cannot *not* label things. Nominalization serves us well: without labels human communications would be impossibly inefficient.

But labels can get us into trouble. For one thing, the descriptive capacity of labels can quickly become predictive as well, For example, the word "shy" implies a complex set of inhibitory behaviors, fears, and other barrier elements. People so conditioned tend to stay at home Friday night, refuse to ask attractive strangers for dates, and so on. Our old friend Mary, for example, is someone who might well call herself shy.

Mary is actually labeling a set of processes (staying at home, feeling afraid, and so on), not a collection of things. But when we label processes such as these, they somehow begin to seem more solid, more like "things." They seem to take on a sort of existence all their own, and get locked into a niche. Mary now thinks of herself as a shy person, a role identification that can easily acquire self-fulfilling character. She thinks of herself as shy, accepts being shy, and then begins acting the way shy people are expected to act. She almost feels like she's found an identity after so many years. Life experiences which otherwise might have helped her become bolder have little impact on Mary. For instance, believing she wants to change, she takes several assertiveness training classes. But the training effects don't last long because, as Mary well knows, shy people don't go around acting assertive.

We all use a wide variety of labels to describe the various aspects of our lives and the lives of others. Labeling, among other things, is one of the major contributing dynamics to the process of overgeneralization described earlier. Nominalizations such as "Jewish," "poor," "liberal," "schizophrenic," and untold others keep us locked into self-fulfilling, repetitive patterns we might otherwise have been able to shake.

A variety of strategies can be used in dealing with labeling problems. We will briefly discuss two of them here. *Denominalization* involves removing the negative label, and describing the process it was intended to represent in sensory terms. *Relabeling* involves substituting a label with positive connotations for the counterproductive negative label.

Denominalization

Denominalization is performed in the same manner as barrier analysis. Use the various questioning techniques you learned in Chapter 4 to break descriptive nouns (such as shy) into sequences and patterns tht can be described in see/hear/feel terms. As before, we suggest that you use a self-interviewing technique.

Q1: Specifically, how do you know you're shy?

A1: I act shy. People tell me I'm shy.

Q2: What people, specifically?

A2: Well, Mother for one . . .

Q3: Specifically, what does your mother mean by "shy"?

A3: Well, she knows I never have dates with men . . .

Q4: Do you agree that, "not having dates with men"

is one of the things you mean when you call yourself, "shy"?

A4: Sure! I'd like to go out more, but I'm too shy!

Q5: Fine. Specifically, what else do you mean when you call yourself shy? (And so on.)

Material from the denominalization process can then be used in goal specification, and the barrier analysis process would go on from there.

Relabeling

In relabeling, a new, positive word or phrase is used to replace the old label's negative connotation. For example, a man who is critical of his jealous nature might redefine "jealousy" as "my desire to give all my love to one person." We once persuaded a hypochondriac to refer to himself as a person who had "a well-developed sensitivity to and knowledge about a wide variety of dangerous ailments." Initially, some people are afraid that giving positive connotations to negative patterns will serve to reinforce, and therefore maintain those patterns. However, this isn't usually the case. Jealousy, hypochondriasis, and other reflexive problems often carry with them the additional stigma of self-criticism. The self-criticism, in turn, can itself lead to a wide variety of complicated and difficult barrier programs. When, *as an interim strategy*, we place the barrier pattern in a positive frame, we begin to feel better about ourselves even as we work to modify it.

Similarly, chores and other odious tasks can be redefined as challenges or games. Ever since Tom Sawyer got Aunt Polly's fence whitewashed and his own pockets full of silver by redefining the chore she gave him as a privilege, these types of reframes have been exceedingly popular. We often use chore redefinition as a motivation strategy. For instance, as we sit at our desks writing this book, we challenge ourselves to finish a particular section by a certain time of the day, or before the sun can rise above a certain tree limb. Chore redefinition leads us directly into the next fallacy category.

The Evaluation Fallacy

"There is nothing either good or bad, but thinking makes it so." So wrote William Shakespeare in *Hamlet* (paraphrasing Epictetus, the Greek Stoic), and so do rational therapists strongly contend today. Now, we admit that this viewpoint can be difficult to maintain in the face of serious injury or illness, or when the local constable has just discovered your son's cannabis plantation. In theory, circumstances seem unfortunate only when you compare them to the way that you would like them to be. However, for all practical purposes some experiences are worse than others. As far as we're concerned, sometimes terrible things do happen.

Nevertheless, a great many people react negatively to experiences which, taken in the proper light, could have neutral or even positive implications. To find out whether or not you fall into this category, you might try the following familiar and pleasant experiment. Get yourself a good bottle of wine, a good friend, and a quiet corner. Get comfortable. Drink half the wine (remember to give your friend some). Now look carefully at the bottle, gauge the level of liquid remaining, and ask yourself whether the bottle is half-empty or half-full. Well? Some would say your answer may be an indication of how you tend to evaluate ambiguous conditions. (It may also be an indication of the quality of wine.)

Most people simply are not aware of the degree to which the arbitrary evaluations and judgments they place on themselves and their experiences affect the overall quality of their lives. Specifically, the embedded fallacy pattern is this: *it seems* that the values and judgments one projects onto a particular target mainly reflect the quality of the target being judged. This is simply untrue. Events and experiences are neutral; it is the individual who injects value and meaning into the days and ways of live experiences. How strange and sad, then, that so many people judge themselves on relative scales—"His house is bigger than mine," "I didn't do as well as Father would have liked"—and thus create negative values that limit their capacity for pleasure. But such would seem to be the nature of the human animal.

This book is full of examples of the negative evaluation fallacy. So let's turn our attention to ways in which these patterns can be altered.

Redefining Liabilities as Assets

This is one of the most common and most valuable reframes. Contemporary society being what it is, many of us are taught early to place a great value on being like everyone else. So we see our differences as liabilities; we feel ashamed of them, and hide them if possible. But at best this leaves us inhibited, and at worst can severely mar the quality of our lives. It would be as much to our advantage to redefine our unique characteristics as assets.

If you have a behavioral idiosyncracy or physical characteristic that seems to be getting in your way, see if you can find a means of using it or proudly showing it off instead of hiding it. Sometimes opportunities to do this will occur naturally; in other cases you'll have to work to set them up. Both what you tell yourself about your "liability/asset" and what you do with it are important in the reframing process. Here are a couple of examples.

Milton Erickson* once told a woman who was hypersensitive about a gap between her front teeth to squirt water through that gap at an attractive young man in her office. Being a very conservative proper woman, she was reluctant at first to follow his advice. Finally she decided to give it a try. Evidently her aim was pretty good, because soon after she and the young man began to date. (More importantly, she became much less sensitive about her teeth.)

We recently worked with a young woman who, having obtained an assistant professorship at the University of California, was now afraid she wouldn't be able to make the grade. She felt that, as a young and inexperienced instructor, her evaluations would compare unfavorably to the "old guard" with whom she worked. Then we began to tell her how lucky we thought she was. We told her she literally couldn't lose: if she were given low evaluations it would only reflect on her lack of experience (which no one could fault her for). If she were well-received, she would enjoy that sweetest of all successes: being the victorious underdog. When she began to see herself as a dark horse,

*A marvelous sense of humor and unbelievably well-honed observation skills made the late Dr. Erickson one of the best "reframers" that ever lived. He used a wide range of reframes to induce and utilize hypnotic trances for clinical purposes.

rather than as someone who had to perform or else, she began to loosen up a little. Then, we told her to use her feelings of inadequacy as teaching tools in class. For instance, in a class on introductory psychotherapy, we suggested that she describe her discomfort to the class (rather than trying to hide it and thus be pressuring herself all the more) as an example of how one learns to deal with stressful situations. She did so and, of course, received a lot of positive feedback from her students. A variety of similar reframes and practical exercises (among other things) gradually helped her to learn to handle her new role at Cal with increasing confidence.

Redefining Problems as Opportunities

In the course of emotional reprogramming, you locate specific demands that, when left unsatisfied, upset you. For example, you demand that your husband arrive home on time from work, and become upset when he's late. On the surface of it his lateness is a problem for you. But look at it this way: if he were never late, then you would never get an opportunity to practice emotional reprogramming! So every time he gets home late, he is simply giving you another opportunity to learn and develop a valuable skill. Why, you ought to thank him for coming home late every once in a while, not throw the frying pan at him!

Redefining clinical problems and/or emotional distress as opportunities for growth constitutes one of the most powerful reprogramming strategies we know. The young graduate student who is asked to introduce the keynote speaker for the next symposium and finds himself petrified at the thought, now has the *opportunity* to transcend his fear of public speaking and learn to communicate effectively in front of groups. The aging jock whose wife is insulted by a drunk in a restaurant has the opportunity to experience anger without having to act on it: to practice the skills of "assertive yielding." The young mother who loses her husband and father of her children in an automobile accident has an opportunity (tragic, we admit) to experience intense loss, and then know the sorrows, joys, and learnings of single parenthood.

Many therapists believe that there is a great value in experiencing intense emotional pain. Victor Frankl, the existentialist and founder of the school of logotherapy, believes that, without suffering, life itself has no meaning. Nor is this view peculiar to Western culture. In the Japanese language, the word for "crisis" is composed of two characters: one representing "danger," and the other representing "opportunity." Thus we find that the problem/opportunity reframe does little more than restate a truth the Japanese people have known for millennia: for the individual willing to risk danger, there is tremendous opportunity for growth and change inherent in any behavioral, emotional, or interpersonal problem. When we can begin to recognize that opportunity, we are already on the way to dissolving the problem itself.

The Try-Harder Fallacy

This pattern has been discussed elsewhere, but it's such a common problem that we believe it deserves another look. We were first made aware of this pattern by Paul Watzlawick and his associates at MRI in Palo Alto.

Dr. Watzlawick believes that most clinical and personal problems are actually maintained by the very behaviors that are meant to solve them.* When an individual tries to solve a problem in a particular fashion, and her solution fails, she will generally try harder to solve the problem with the original ineffective solution, rather than look for a new, possibly more appropriate strategy. For example, the stutterer tries not to stutter. In so doing, she becomes so tense that she stutters all the more. The insomniac tries as hard as he can to get to sleep at night; and of course succeeds only in becoming wider and wider awake.

A clarification may be in order here. We have nothing against diligent, motivated efforts to solve problems. Individuals become trapped in the try-harder fallacy only when they become locked into repeating ineffective tactics over and over again. Unfortunately, this happens all the time.

The Linear Growth Fallacy

The linear growth fallacy derives from life-long exposure to a culture which operates on the principle that the shortest distance between two poles is a straight line. It's natural (for those of us so trained) to imagine that the path of self-actualization, of personal growth, is also relatively linear. It's even more natural to believe that the actualized being, the seeker who has found enlightenment, the master, is very different from we mere mortals who are still struggling along.

---

*For additional information on the work of this very creative group, see Watzlawick, P., Weakland, J., and Fisch, R. *Change*. Palo Alto, Science and Behavior Books, 1974.

First, the path to enlightenment happens to be any-thing but linear. In fact (sticking with our simplistic, two-dimensional metaphor), it may resemble nothing so much as a horseshoe. Conditions of "low enlightenment" and "high enlightenment" in some ways turn out to be very close to one another. For instance, Allan Watts was fond of talking about the "low outcast" and the "high outcast." The former is someone who fails to function effectively in society. He is cast out, and must live as best he can on society's fringe. He may become a hobo, or move to a place like the Haight-Ashbury district in San Francisco to live with others of his kind. The high outcast, on the other hand, rejects society. He has plenty of ability to "make it," but he chooses to march to a different drummer instead. And he too may well wind up being a hobo or living in a one-room flat on the Haight. From within society, say, from the point of view of the tourist from Milwaukee, these two individuals may look very much alike. They may be so similar in dress, talk, and behavior that the tourist would be hard pressed to tell them apart. Of course, at another level they're as different as night and day. One is a robot, and a badly-programmed robot at that. The other is free.

Similarly, consider three men standing side by side in a bar. Each is challenged by a drunken bully to fight. The first man is a coward. Fear paralyzes him. He can do nothing but hang his head and with lowered eyes, scurry out of the bar. The second man used to play football in college; and aside from a burgeoning spare tire around his middle, has kept himself in reasonable shape. He doesn't run away, not him! He meets the bully head-on, with words, and if necessary, with his fists as well.

The third man standing at the bar has a black belt in a martial art such as Aikido or Karate. He has trained for years, and has the physical ability to break his antagonist into many rather small pieces without really thinking about it. He certainly doesn't fear the bully—but neither does he have anything to prove. So, if at all possible, the black belt will probably choose to bow silently to the other man, finish his drink, and leave the bar. To a bar full of bullies and aging college football players, his behavior may look a lot like that of a coward. But again, the first man is a slave and the third one a master.

Very high levels and very low levels of awareness, actualization, growth, and "being" may look similar in many ways. But it usually proves impossible to go directly from one to the other, to take a "shortcut." The path of actualization, the path from slavery to mastery, will undoubtedly lead you far and wide before it brings you back home.

This brings us to another point: though high levels and low levels look the same, medium levels often appear startlingly different. Recall Siddartha, who left a simple life to roam the world searching for meaning and truth. He eventually came to the big city and, being a smart lad, quickly learned the ways of the businessman. Soon he became rich and perfumed and fat, as he lived a life diametrically opposed to the one he had left. Yet the city life of gluttony and sin turned out to be empty for him as well. He grew hopeless, and went to the river to drown himself. But what he found as he looked into the waters and contemplated his own death helped him transcend the trappings of wealth and power and continue on his path to meaning. By the end of the book Siddartha has returned to the simple life and is living in a style very similar to the one he'd originally left. Of course, in his "sameness" there was a tremendous difference as well.

On a practical level, the linear growth fallacy is this: people tend to define the "shortest distance" to actualization, or fulfillment, as a straight line. They begin the journey and manage to reach the "middle levels" as did Siddartha. Now they are effective, well-programmed robots, instead of badly-programmed, ineffective ones. But there they stop. They strive for riches, power, and sexual conquest—and many of them do reach these goals. But somehow the victory is a hollow one. They have defined the middle levels and the advantages to be had there as ends in themselves rather than as stations or paths leading to a deeper, fuller end.

Unsatisfied yet not understanding, they *try harder*. More riches, more power, more sex. Yet still they remain unsatisfied, certain needs remain unfulfilled. So they try harder still. These people have become mired in the various traps and paradoxes that accompany success; and they don't know how to move on.

The linear growth fallacy is a tough pattern to break. Except to suggest continued awareness and vigilance, we have no particular programming strategy to offer. Frankly, we are inexperienced in this area, and are not sure how skilled even we ourselves might be at transcending barriers such as riches, power, and sex. (Though we do hope at some point to have the opportunity to try.) We figure we'll deal with that particular bridge if, as, and when we come to it. It is certainly a span many travelers never do manage to cross.

SUMMARY

In this chapter we've attempted to describe eight patterns of thinking, eight viewpoint characteristics, that tend to get people into trouble. These are:

1) "either-or" reasoning
2) "if-then" reasoning
3) the Golden Rule
4) generalization
5) nominalization (labeling)
6) evaluation
7) trying harder
8) the assumption of "linear growth"

These and other common characteristics of thoughts and beliefs can lead to circular reasoning and the formation of barrier systems that are as resistant to change as they are inhibiting to spontaneity and growth.

Modifying belief systems is a two-step process. First, find the fallacy or fallacies imbedded in the structure of the belief system. Then reframe your perspective. That is, replace the fallacy pattern with a viewpoint or perspective that makes it easier, rather than harder, for you to reach your goals. This doesn't necessarily mean that, after reframing, you will be viewing the world "the way it really is." A great many people from physicists to philosophers agree that the way the world "really is" is largely (or entirely) a matter of perspective. Rather, now you will be viewing the world in a way that works for you. What we've called "fallacy patterns" aren't necessarily wrong. Rather, they are viewpoint structures that commonly keep people from getting what they say they want. Effective reframing will allow you to construct belief systems that are consistent with the goal-directed behavior and generally positive attitude that you've hoped to learn from reading this book. We repeat, your new perspectives will be more operational, but they won't necessarily be more "right." We suggest that, in your newfound wisdom and enlightenment, you not go out and try to sell them to other people. Remember the Golden Rule Fallacy: different people have varying needs, styles, and goals. Your newfound beliefs may not serve them as well as their own do. As with most everything else, the most salient characteristic of a "good" belief system is that it works to help you optimize your threescore-and-ten on this planet, while not keeping other people from optimizing theirs.

AFTERWORD

This book is a training guide designed to help readers deal with conflicting feelings and ineffective behavior during stress situations. These barrier systems are learned patterns of behavior and experience that get in the way and keep you from getting all there is to get out of life. Just as the mind and body can be likened to a flesh-and-blood computer, these complex sequences are similar to computer programs that operate to lead you away from, rather than toward, your goals. In Chapter 1 we describe the ways in which these programs work, and survey the various sensory and behavioral elements that make them up. We also see how the sequences can loop back on themselves and form self-propagating, self-rewarding vicious circles that are as unpleasant as they are difficult to break. Understanding the nature of barrier systems is the first step in breaking free of their influence and so our book begins with this process of self examination.

Barrier analysis itself is a three-step process involving goal-setting, barrier specification, and conflict resolution.

Being vague or confused about what you wish to accomplish is one of the best ways we know to fail to accomplish anything. Long-term, complicated, hazy goals are much easier to avoid than are immediate, specific ones. For that reason barrier analysis calls for clear, systematic goal-setting.

When your goals are clarified it's time to explore the patterns that are stopping you from reaching them. This is done simultaneously on four "logical levels" of experience. On a behavioral level, how do you act that may be getting in your way? What difficult situations do you have to contend with? On the perceptual plane, what do you see, hear, feel, taste, or smell that may be keeping you from your goal? Conceptually, what do you remember? Anticipate? Say to yourself? Finally, what beliefs may be involved? That is, do you have any value systems or points of view that may be making your goal difficult to work toward and attain? These are the elements that form the complex patterns we call barrier systems.

We assume that most people already have most of the skills they need to reach the goals they set for themselves. Certainly skill training (management seminars, assertion training, tennis lessons, whatever) is important. But we know people who attend management seminars regularly, and still become defensive or critical or simply ineffective as soon as the going in the office gets tough. This is where reprogramming comes in. Dissolve the barriers and you will attain your goals.

However, before attempting to dissolve anything it's important to take a look at what your barriers may be doing *for* you. The most annoying of barrier patterns usually serve or once served a practical purpose. Thus you may feel some conflict about giving them up no matter how debilitating they've become. In Chapter 4 we introduce a process to help you explore and, if possible, resolve inner conflict. It can also help you distinguish between goals you really do want to reach and ones about which you honestly haven't yet made up your mind. Then you can reconfirm a commitment to the former while laying aside the others for the time being.

The change strategies presented in Section II fall into three general categories: sequencing, duplication, and reframing. Sequence reprogramming involves using simple learning theory principles like association and reward to connect positive, useful reactions to barrier sequences.

It may seem paradoxical, but one of the best ways to break a bad habit is to practice, and often to exaggerate, the very behaviors you would like to change. 'Similis simula curantur" is a Greek phrase often ascribed to Aristotle which, roughly translated, means, "Like cures like." Systematic, repeated exposure to feared situations, for instance, often serves to reduce the intensity of the fear. The behavioral technique called "symptom prescription" involves having a stutterer stammer intentionally—eventually this may help him become more fluent. A variety of these duplication tactics are described in Chapter 6.

Psychologists generally agree that assumptions we make and viewpoints we adopt influence the quality of life a lot more than most people realize. Some people habitually evaluate ambiguous circumstances in a negative manner: they see a half glass of wine as half empty rather than half full. To them, every silver lining must have a cloud! Others make assumptions that needlessly limit their options or consistently lead to negative outcomes. It is a most valuable skill (and really more an art than a science) to be able to reframe values, viewpoints, and assumptions in ways that help us deal with the world more effectively and feel more positive about ourselves and our lives.

Overcoming Your Barriers was first published in workbook form in 1977. We used it as a therapeutic training aid and to supplement our professional seminars. The book itself was begun at the request of students and colleagues who wished a fuller presentation of the barriers material. We still use it as a therapy/study guide for our clients and students. A great many colleagues have told us they also find it a valuable aid in their clinical work. And, of course, we believe the book stands on its own as a practical self-help/self-study manual.

This is the end of our journey together—but, hopefully, just the first of many trips you'll be taking on the highways and byways of barrier analysis. You've read through the book, and probably you've experimented with some of the ideas it contains. Now comes the test! Now it's time for what, in our workshops, we call "training for effect." The concepts have been presented. The demonstrations are finished. All that is left is to roll up your sleeves, pick a place to start, and get to work.

The exercises described in this book are conceptually innovative, are easy to learn, and (usually) work. But there are no panaceas hidden in these pages, no quick fixes. Barrier analysis takes work, time, and a deep commitment to persevere. If you have those, we trust you will find the procedures invaluable in exploring the habits, feelings, beliefs and other patterns which interfere with your productivity. By Overcoming Your Barriers you can respond to stress in a positive way and reach your real goals.

SUGGESTED READING

Bach, G. R. and R. M. Deutsch. *Stop! You're Driving Me Crazy*. New York: Putnam, 1979.

Bach, R. *Illusions: The Adventure of a Reluctant Messiah*. New York: Delacorte Press, 1977.

Bandler, R. and J. Grinder. *The Structure of Magic, Vol. 1*. Cupertino, CA: Science and Behavior Books, 1975.

Dobson, T. and V. Miller. *Giving In To Get Your Way*. New York: Delacorte, 1978.

Ellis, A. *Reason and Emotion in Psychotherapy*. New York: Lyle Stewart, 1962.

Erickson, M. H. and Rossi, E. L. *Hypnotic Realities*. New York: Irvington Press, 1978.

Fay, A. *Making Things Better by Making Them Worse*. New York: Hawthorne Books, 1978.

Gendlin, E. T. *Focusing*. New York: Everest House, 1978.

Greenberg, D. *How To Make Yourself Miserable: A Vital Training Manual*. New York: Random House, 1966.

Hampden-Turner, C. *Maps of the Mind*. New York: Macmillan Publishing Company, 1981.

Hayakawa, S. I. *Language in Thought and Action*. New York: Harcourt, Brace, and World, 1964.

Hofsladter, D. R. and D. C. Dennett. *The Mind's Eyes: Fantasies and Reflections on Self and Soul*. New York: Bantam Books, 1982.

Jung, C. Forward to the *I Ching*. In *I Ching or Book of Changes* (Richard Wilhelm translation). Princeton, N.J.: Princeton University Press, 1967, xxi-xxxix.

Kopp, S. *If You Meet the Buddha On the Road, Kill Him!* Cupertino: Science and Behavior Books, 1972.

Lazarus, A. A. and A. Fay. *I Can If I Want To*. New York: William Morrow & Co., 1975.

Lazarus, A. A. *In the Mind's Eye*. New York: Rawson Publishers, 1977.

Leonard, G. *The Ultimate Athlete*. New York: Viking Press, 1975.

Piaget, G. W. and Barbara Binkley. *Barriers To Change: A Training Workbook*. Portola Valley, CA: IAHB Press, 1981.

Piaget, G. W. and Barbara Binkley. *How To Communicate Under Pressure: Dealing Effectively with Difficult People*. Portola Valley: IAHB Press, 1982.

Simonton, O. C., Stephanie Matthews-Simonton, and J. L. Creighton. *Getting Well Again*. New York: Bantam Books, 1980.

Watzlawick, P., J. Weakland, and R. Fisch. *Change*. Palo Alto: Science and Behavior Books, 1974.

Zukov, G. *The Dancing Wu-Li Masters*. New York: Morrow Quill Paperbacks, 1978.